SECOND EDITION
GROUP EXERCISES FOR ADOLESCENTS

Be a part of improving group work for adolescents everywhere, and get your contribution published!

If selected, your group exercise will appear in the upcoming *MORE Group Exercises For Adolescents: A Manual For Therapists.*

Here's how:

Send your favorite tried-and-true group exercise to the author (address follows). It will be tested and if selected will be included in the new manual along with your name, occupation, degree, place of employment (or college or university if a student), address, and (if desired) phone and e-mail address.

Send exercises to

Carrell Counseling, P.C.
1200 E. Woodhurst
Building S, Suite 400
Springfield, MO 65804

SECOND EDITION

GROUP EXERCISES FOR ADOLESCENTS

A MANUAL FOR THERAPISTS

SUSAN CARRELL

Sage Publications, Inc.
International Educational and Professional Publisher
Thousand Oaks ■ London ■ New Delhi

For information:

Sage Publications, Inc.
2455 Teller Road
Thousand Oaks, California 91320
E-mail: order@sagepub.com

Sage Publications Ltd.
6 Bonhill Street
London EC2A 4PU
United Kingdom

Sage Publications India Pvt. Ltd.
M-32 Market
Greater Kailash I
New Delhi 110 048 India

Printed in the United States of America

Library of Congress Cataloging-in-Publication Data

Carrell, Susan.
  Group exercises for adolescents: A manual for therapists / by
Susan Carrell. — 2nd ed.
    p. cm.
  Includes bibliographical references (p.).
  ISBN 0-7619-1953-8
  2. Group psychotherapy for teenagers Problems, exercises, etc.
I. Title.
  RJ505.G7 C37 2000
  616.89'152'0835—dc21   99-6772

        04 05 10 9 8 7 6 5 4 3 2

Acquiring Editor:	Marquita Flemming
Editorial Assistant:	Anna Howland
Production Editor:	Diana E. Axelsen
Editorial Assistant:	Cindy Bear
Typesetter/Designer:	Janelle Lemaster
Cover Designer:	Michelle Lee

CONTENTS

● ● ● ● ● ● ● ● ● ● ● ● ● ● ● ● ●

PREFACE

● ● ● ● ● ● ● ● ● ● ● ● ● ● ● ● ●

I wrote this book because I needed it so badly myself. When I began doing group therapy with hospitalized adolescents, I inherited two or three "exercises" from colleagues who preceded me. The difference in the way the teenagers responded when I used these structured activities instead of just allowing the group to generate their own agenda was dramatic. I discovered that the structure an exercise provided became a jumping-off place that enabled adolescents to disclose emotional material that was otherwise very difficult to unearth. I learned that if properly conceived, a group exercise would open emotional doors in a safe and nonthreatening way. It also became clear that group members had more fun and felt more at ease when an exercise was used. So I began trying to find more. It was not an easy task. I found few exercises in books that seemed right for the population with whom I worked. Most were too immature because they were developed either for children or for low-functioning, chronically ill individuals. Few had the sophistication or relevance that would interest a savvy group of teens. My quest began in earnest. After several years, I had a collection that worked. Only I could never find them. The exercise I needed would be at home in my desk or had been loaned to a colleague and never returned. Or I would plan a certain exercise, only to have my disgruntled group announce that we had done that one three sessions ago. So I had to do something. I also was becoming convinced that other therapists needed and deserved the fruits of my collecting and creating.

I learned that working with adolescents in groups was a whole different ball game than doing group therapy with adults. Resistance is often prevalent and powerful in adolescent groups. However, the need for peer approval and acceptance is equally strong. The challenge to the therapist is to overcome resistance and to harness peer acceptance for use in meeting therapeutic goals. I found the challenge energizing and intoxicating. This manual is an offering to those who, like myself, are irresistibly drawn to the wonder and excitement of working with adolescents in groups.

ACKNOWLEDGMENTS

My thanks and love to the people who made this book possible: My parents, Ralph and Mildred Gilbert, who enabled me to love teenagers by giving me a safe and healthy adolescence.

My children, Matthew and Emily, who, during their adolescence, shared my time and attention with so many others.

My professor, Shirley Hendricks, who encouraged me to follow my dreams and allowed me to do so in her courses.

My friend and mentor, Paula Caplan, who gave and gave and gave.

My supervisor, Kathy Forson, who believed in me and fought the system in my behalf.

My friend, Carole Riesenberg, who sacrificed her own busy schedule to edit for me.

My editor, Marquita Flemming, who said "YES!" and stuck by me.

Winston Davis, my true companion in this and everything else. And Barbara Jenkins, the faithful friend who typed the pages and organized my efforts.

The acknowledgments just listed were for the first edition of this book, and they stand. My gratitude for this second edition goes to all those therapist-types who bought the book to use with their groups. The purchase of the first edition for use in your agency, hospital, group home, detention center, school, residential facility, and private practice has made this new and expanded edition possible. In addition, I am grateful for your contact with me by phone or letter to ask questions or make comments and suggestions. Hopefully, I have improved the book's usefulness because of the information exchanged.

I would like to thank Kassie Gavrilis, my editor for this edition, for her support and encouragement along the way. Her steady, calm nature was a great source of comfort.

My thanks to Maggie Megalynn, my colleague and dear friend who masterminded our great escapes—the writing retreats that gave me a space in which to complete this project.

Winston Davis, now my husband, continues to be my true companion in this and everything else.

INTRODUCTION
USING THE MANUAL

FEAST OR FAMINE

Some therapists say that doing group therapy with adolescents is no picnic, but others claim it is the icing on the cake. Most acknowledge it is an essential part of a balanced therapeutic diet.

This manual is more a menu planner than a cookbook, offering an array of selections that create an attractive, as well as nourishing, menu for the troubled teenager. Although the basic meals are planned, there is ample room for the signature of the therapist who prepares them. The individuality of the therapist's own seasoning and presentation makes each experience unique. Similarly, alterations in the manual (such as the order of exercises you use) may be made to fit the needs of the school, agency, or other institution.

Group leaders should feel free to cater to the appetites of their groups or to their own tastes when planning each session. The activities do not need to be followed in the order of their appearance in the manual; for example, one week an exercise from the section "Living With Family" may be chosen, whereas the next week's selection might come from the section "Living With Discovery."

The 31-week curriculum presupposes a once-a-week therapy experience. However, if you need a daily group session for 3 weeks (or 2 or even 1), the manual has it; just choose which exercise you want each day.

The materials required for each session usually are provided with the exercise. For several, however, you will need to acquire some materials before the session. Those materials involve minimal expenditure and should not threaten the budget of any institution, agency, or individual.

Advance preparation by leader or member is seldom required. When it is, look to the "Method" section of the exercise. It is best to read through all of the exercises before you use the curriculum for the first time. You then can determine the order in which you want to proceed, the materials you need to gather or purchase, and the exercises that require some advance preparation. Of course, when you are actually working with a group, it is important to be sensitive to topics generated in one session that might point the way to selection of the next exercise. Another option is to use an exercise periodically. I did one group in a school setting this way. The participants in the group often needed to talk about classroom and school issues, so we used a structured exercise during every other group session. You may have a direction in mind, or you may choose to follow the order of exercises in the manual, but being ready to make changes according to the needs and interests of the group is essential.

SINK OR SWIM

Whether by choice or by chance, and at some point in their careers, most mental health professionals who work with teens experience the "call" to lead group therapy sessions. A plunge into the waters of group therapy with adolescents can make for an exhilarating swim or a frustrating, exhausting struggle. This manual is intended to provide support for therapists in meeting the challenge.

The curriculum for group experiences offered here may be used exactly as presented or altered to meet the needs of the particular institution, school, agency, or therapist. The purpose of the manual is to provide the mental health professional a strategy for working with adolescents in the group setting.

This is a how-to, hands-on manual for the busy therapist. It is assumed that the therapist using this manual understands basic techniques for leading groups and has knowledge and experience specific to adolescents. I hope the manual will be useful to veteran clinicians, while offering a foundation for those newer to the field.

BEGGED, BORROWED, OR STOLEN

The curriculum of exercises in this manual was developed during many years of trial and error. The exercises chosen are more the result of evolution than of selection. Most were borrowed from the work of colleagues, some were taken from workshops and seminars with slight alterations, and a few I created. This manual is the result of collecting, trying, critiquing, and cataloging each exercise. To my knowledge, none has been lifted from material or texts under copyright.

Good group activities circulate among professionals like good jokes among friends. One struggles to remember just how that group activity was constructed or what successful group exercise was shared by a colleague at that conference last fall. This manual describes and organizes such material.

A study of the curriculum also was conducted. At a hospital-based psychiatric unit for adolescents, 305 patients were asked to fill out questionnaires after participating in groups in which the curriculum was used. The adolescents were of both sexes, aged 11 to 18. The groups were open; that is, patients came into and left the curriculum as they were admitted and discharged from the institution.

Participants answered questionnaires at the end of each group exercise. Anonymity of respondents was assured each week in an attempt to encourage honest responses. The survey form (p. 4) used a Likert scale, and a mean analysis was performed on the data collected (Carrell, 1991).

Results reflected the developmental concerns of adolescence. The favorite exercises were those in which peer interaction was the prevalent theme. The less a leader was involved, the higher an exercise was rated by the teens. Favored exercises cast the leader in the role of benevolent coach, encouraging and supporting participation in the group activity. Less enthusiastically received exercises put the leader in a more formal teaching role.

A number of exercises were such abysmal failures that they were eliminated before the data were analyzed. Those that failed did not capture the teens' interest; either the subject was not pertinent or the format for the exercise lacked appeal.

Exercises that were not described as fun but that seemed necessary were left in the curriculum because they provide information needed by most troubled teens. For example, "The Loss Cycle" exercise is not exciting and fun, but an understanding of the phases of grieving has been a turning point in the course of recovery for many teens and thus remains in the curriculum.

The survey forms included a space for respondents to suggest topics, but no topic was mentioned that was not already included in the curriculum. The topic most frequently requested was sex.

Table I.1.   Between Teens Group: A Patient Satisfaction Survey

The topic for today was _____

_____

1 = Strongly Disagree   2 = Disagree   3 = No Opinion   4 = Agree   5 = Strongly Agree

1. I liked group today.	1	2	3	4	5
2. I figured out something about myself in group today.	1	2	3	4	5
3. I figured out something about my family in group today.	1	2	3	4	5
4. I learned something about another group member.	1	2	3	4	5
5. I felt comfortable in this group.	1	2	3	4	5
6. I shared something about myself in group.	1	2	3	4	5
7. I felt supported by the group leader.	1	2	3	4	5
8. I had fun in group.	1	2	3	4	5
9. I am looking forward to next week's group.	1	2	3	4	5
10. I talked in group today.	1	2	3	4	5

A topic I would like the group to discuss is _____

_____

TURF AND TERRITORY

Turf and territory issues between disciplines are all too familiar in the mental health professions. Basically, we all own the same land. Some of us fence it, some cultivate it, some mow it, some analyze its composition, and some re-create on it. Our different perspectives ensure that the land is used to the fullest. Counselors, psychiatrists, juvenile officers, nurses, recreation therapists, social workers, psychologists, mental health technicians, occupational therapists, and music and art therapists all do group work with adolescents. There is room for all of us.

I once worked in a psychiatric hospital where only social workers were allowed to do group therapy—ridiculous! I worked in another where only psychiatrists did group work—equally ridiculous!

Hospitalized and institutionalized teens need as much therapy as possible. Third-party payment vendors are beginning to demand it. One therapy group a day for hospitalized adolescents is not enough. This curriculum can stand alone as the group therapy experience for teens in outpatient settings such as private practice clinics or schools, but it serves equally well as one of several group modalities in inpatient settings. Objectives identified at the beginning of each exercise should be helpful to those clinicians developing treatment plans for their clients or patients.

There is really no room for the fear that spawns territorial conflict among mental health professionals; troubled teens need us all.

THE BIG PICTURE

The curriculum was designed to address five goals:

1. Develop a sense of belonging to a group
2. Decrease feelings of uniqueness
3. Increase self-confidence
4. Enhance insight
5. Increase self-awareness

Each exercise identifies specific objectives that move group members toward attainment of these more global goals.

THE BASIC PATTERN: ONE SIZE FITS ALL

Whether your group is in a hospital or a classroom, this pattern will fit:

A. Seating arrangement should be in a circle. Sitting around a table is not recommended: The table can serve as a barrier that inhibits openness and intimacy. The group circle, whether on the floor or in chairs or on couches or on bean bags, is a signature of group therapy and sets the experience apart from other activities. If the use of a table is required by the exercise (e.g., when group members write or draw on a worksheet), move the group to the table or tables to do their work and then bring group members back together in the circle to share and process.

B. The round-robin method of sharing is effective in adolescent groups. Teens are not skilled in social intercourse, and unstructured interaction can be threatening. In round-robin, each member knows when it is his or her turn to speak; it also ensures the leader's control of the length of time allotted to each member. The leader can change this format at any time, with any exercise, to encourage practice of spontaneous interaction in the group setting.

C. The Group Statement (p. 39) should be read at the beginning of each group session. The therapist may choose a member to read it each time, the group may elect a member each time, or the leader may ask for a volunteer. Ownership of the group experience is reiterated in the Group Statement, and the rules are defined. It is an effective way to bring the focus of the group to the task at hand.

NAMING THE GROUP

Between Teens Group is the name suggested in the manual. This name was chosen because it emphasizes teen-to-teen relationships. What you call your group, however, is up to you. You may come up with a name that is more descriptive of your group's membership—Discovery Group or Self-Esteem Group, for example. Or you may want to have your group decide on a name themselves. That in itself would be an interesting group exercise. I have used Between Teens Group in hospitals and in schools. It seems to work well, and most people like it.

PART

1

ADOLESCENCE
THE DEVELOPMENTAL BLUEPRINT

BETWEEN A ROCK AND A HARD PLACE:
THE TERRIBLE TWOS AND THE TERRIBLE TEENS

Some people think all teenagers are emotionally disordered. Really, teenagers are just busy. The developmental tasks of adolescence are demanding enough in and of themselves; add the demands of a complex society, and it is no wonder so many become overwhelmed. When healthy coping mechanisms go into overload and fail, symptoms of distress begin to show. Alcohol and drug abuse, suicide attempts, stealing and shoplifting, school difficulties, sexual acting out, depression or mania, violent outbursts, running away from home or school, and creating chaos within the family are common reactions to a sense of overwhelming anxiety.

Before presenting the exercises for teen groups, I briefly review the developmental tasks of adolescence because these tasks form the stage on which the experience of group therapy is performed.

DEVELOPMENTAL TASKS OF ADOLESCENCE

1. Separation/Individuation

Separation and individuation are the most important tasks of adolescence. The separation issue, with its inherent abandonment and engulfment themes, produces a wealth of bizarre manifestations: the 13-year-old girl who runs away from home so that she will get caught, the 14-year-old boy who steals money from the father he fears but idolizes, the overachieving 15-year-old who excels at basketball and attempts suicide before the big game, the academically gifted 16-year-old who is flunking out of school, and the 17-year-old with wealthy parents who shoplifts; the list goes on.

Developmentally, adolescence brings a second shot at separation. The last time this struggle ensued was around age 2 ("the terrible twos"), and every parent who survived remembers. The dynamics during adolescence are not so different. When frustrated parents lament that their troubled teen behaves just like a 2-year-old, you might want to be sympathetic and assure them they could not be more right!

The similarity of separation issues of the twos and the teens is displayed in Table 1.1.

TABLE 1.1   A Comparison of Twos and Teens

Twos	*Teens*
1. Rebel against parental requests	1. Rebel against parental requests
2. Are "fearfully fascinated" with peers	2. Are "fearfully fascinated" with peers
3. Need constant reassurance of parental presence (i.e., "quietly available" parents)	3. Need constant reassurance of parental presence (i.e., "quietly available" parents)
4. Issues of control:	4. Issues of control:
a. Toilet training	a. Curfew setting
b. The clenched teeth of 18-month-olds who will not eat	b. The defiant refusal of 14-year-olds to talk to their parents
5. Will not share toys	5. Will not share boyfriends or girlfriends (guard love relationships possessively)
6. Struggle to dominate in play	6. Struggle to dominate in peer approval
7. Put things into their mouths, from buttons to bugs	7. Put things into their mouths, from alcohol to drugs

2. Developing a Consistent Identity

Adolescents try on identities like so many changes of clothes. Unfortunately, some of these costumes depict unsavory, even dangerous, lifestyles. One cannot help but be concerned about the young person who identifies with those in the drug culture or the occult. Other capricious flirtations with the wild side can have disastrous consequences.

Less dramatic identity struggles have equal emotional weight. The belligerent rebel who "smart-mouths" all of his or her teachers, the class clown with deep-seated feelings of inferiority, and the overweight 12-year-old in special learning classes all wonder who they are and what they are worth. The musically untalented girl who dreams of being a rock star, or the boy who barely passes his classes but insists he will go to medical school like his grandfather, has dreams way out of synch with reality.

Developing a solid sense of self is a painful process. Even the best adjusted adolescents must walk through the fires of self-discovery.

3. Developing a Peer-Group Identity

As important as the question Who am I? is the question Where do I fit in? Peer acceptance and identification with a group are the most compelling concerns of adolescence. To teens, the need for peer acceptance far exceeds self-esteem needs. Parents and teachers beg the question when they ask, "How could you allow them to treat you like that" or "Can't you see they're just using you?" It is hard for adults to remember how powerful the need for acceptance can be.

Forming a satisfying peer group identity may be the hub of the developmental wheel for adolescents. All other developmental tasks are inextricably tied to this one.

4. Attainment of Sexual Identity

Gender identity comes during childhood. Adolescent girls already have all sorts of notions about what being female means. Likewise, adolescent boys know for sure they are boys and have lots of ideas about what that means. The identity of a sexual self, and the expression of that self, begins in adolescence.

For some teens, discovery of their own sexuality and attraction to the other sex is as natural as growing. It is not really anything you think about; it just happens. For others, coming to grips with sexual identity is an elusive prize, just out of reach.

Normal sexual fantasies loom like sinister demons in secret thought. Unspoken fears remain unexplored, and frightening questions go unanswered—and often unasked. One sexual fantasy, a single attraction, or a solitary experience can permanently scar an unenlightened adolescent. These are fragile times.

5. Development of a Personal Value System

Until adolescence, children adopt the value systems of their parents. Then, all hell breaks loose. Previously held beliefs, mores, values, and standards are all up for grabs. The tranquil waters of family life may become a turbulent sea. The boat rocks.

This does not mean that everything, or even anything, will change; it does mean that it all may be questioned.

The black and white of right and wrong begin to take on shades of gray as moral development evolves.

Unfortunately, many adolescents do not emerge from childhood with a well-defined value system from their families. Developmentally, there is not much time left. Who will shape the morality of these children? Teachers, coaches, school counselors, juvenile authorities, therapists, and other authority figures face a formidable task.

6. Development of Life Goals for the Future

Most children do not decide what work they are going to do when they grow up until very late adolescence. Our educational system, however, pushes adolescents toward defining career goals before they enter high school. High school curriculums may place students into "collegiate" or "vocational" tracks as soon as their freshman years.

Many individuals enter the paid work force for the first time when they get summer jobs during their high school years. The world of finance becomes real when a teenager obtains a car and must maintain the vehicle with his or her own money.

Teens explore a variety of interests through elective courses during high school. Special-interest clubs and organizations offer other new territories to explore. Life experiences, academic performance, and innate abilities merge during adolescence to define a career direction.

THE PUSH-PULL OF ADOLESCENCE

Adolescence takes dichotomy to new heights. Slogans like "biting the hand that feeds you" and "shooting yourself in the foot" come to mind. Teens rebel against the very things they need. It is the "normal" condition of adolescents—indeed, it is their job. Our job, as adults and therapists, is to remember that and to react accordingly.

One of the most helpful interventions I know when a teen is caught in the push-pull of his or her own contradictions is to explain it. It does not take much: "Of course, you hate your mother's demands to know where you are going; it's your job in life to hate it. Your mother's job is to demand to know. Looks to me like you're both doing your jobs well." Or "Tyler, I understand you needed to test the limits in group yesterday; you're 13 years old, and it's your job to test limits. It's my job to set and enforce limits; so that's why I kicked you out."

These explanations are empowering. You know how it feels to be lost in a large shopping mall and discover one of those directories that point out "You are here"; your situation becomes much less ominous! Teens are relieved when you tell them their behavior is age appropriate. Of course, most of us work with teens whose behavior is extreme. Point out this difference and remind them that is why they are where they are—hospital, mental health agency, detention center, outpatient clinic, or wherever. Remind them it is possible for them to struggle with the issues that all teens confront without getting themselves into so much trouble. The clearest example for them concerns limits. Most teens will acknowledge that setting and enforcing limits is a sign of caring.

FIVE POLARITIES OF ADOLESCENCE

1. Rebellion for adult control/need for direction:

   Good decisions come from experience; experience comes from bad decisions. Adults must be involved when teens make bad decisions and help them learn from those mistakes. Teens must have enough freedom to be able to make some bad decisions!

2. Wish for closeness/fear of intimacy:

   Teens would like to have close relationships with others, even adult authority figures; but they are suspicious. Do others really have their best interests at heart? Will they be understood and accepted? What is required of them in a close and personal relationship?

3. Push and test limits/see limits as sign of caring:

   The "structure" or "system," meaning family, school, church, inpatient environment, and so forth, must be stronger than the teen who tests it. It is a basic ingredient of security for a developing adult.

4. Think of future/oriented to present:

   A college-bound teen may *know* that consistently good academic performance is required in order to get accepted to college but won't get off the phone long enough to study.

5. Sexually mature/cognitively not ready to experience sexuality (Scheidlinger, 1991):

   Teenagers will engage in sexual behavior; however, as much as they might want it, teens should not have sexual intercourse. There are a number of reasons, but the most compelling seems to be that they are not emotionally prepared to handle the break-ups that so predictably occur.

P A R T

2

GROUP THERAPY
WITH ADOLESCENTS

BY HOOK OR BY CROOK: WHY DO GROUPS?

The challenge of working with adolescents in therapy is engaging them. The majority of adults enter therapy willingly and of their own volition, but teenagers often are coerced into treatment against their wishes. Their parents, the school, or the courts insist they attend therapy sessions. It is up to the therapist to "hook" the reluctant adolescent into real participation in the therapeutic experience.

It is the nature of human beings to form groups. It is the sine qua non of adolescents to form groups. This is the hook to engagement in therapy. Peer relationships are the crux of most adolescents' concerns. The majority of their time, attention, interest, and energy is devoted to issues related to peers. Group therapy capitalizes on this developmental principle by serving up what teens most desire yet most fear—peer interaction.

Historically, mental health professionals have debated about the most effective type of group therapy. Likewise, group leaders' styles, approaches, and degrees of involvement have been the subjects of numerous surveys and studies. This manual allows facilitators to incorporate their own therapeutic styles and theoretical convictions with the exercises provided. Leaders are encouraged to think of themselves as benevolent "coaches," encouraging self-disclosure and exchange of conversation between group members while providing emotional support. The leader's principal role is to hook group members' interest and involvement in each exercise and then to set them free to interact with each other.

For several reasons, working with adolescents in groups is better than working with them in individual therapy alone (Berkovitz & Sugar, 1975):

1. *Group therapy challenges the myth of uniqueness.* Young people often feel as if no one else has the feelings they have, has experienced what they have, or understands what they are going through. The discovery that others have indeed shared in these emotions and experiences is empowering, especially if those acknowledging similar feelings and thoughts are their peers.

2. *Group therapy provides the adult leadership adolescents want, while allowing them to assert their own power and independence.* The group becomes a stage where issues of dependence and independence are rehearsed. The leader's authority is firm enough to provide an atmosphere of safety but soft enough to foster the teens' self-reliance. In the context of group therapy, the adolescent finds the freedom to practice independent behavior within the safety of the structure provided by the leader.

3. *Group therapy reduces the discomfort in the adult-child dynamic of individual therapy.* The one-to-one relationship of client and therapist in individual therapy is uncomfortable, even threatening, to many young people because they have had poor relationships with other adult authority figures. Their bonding with their parents has been inadequate for a number of reasons, and they often have had bad experiences with teachers, law enforcement officials, case workers, and the like. In their eyes, adults may be "the enemy." The balance of power provided by the group defuses the climate of distrust and fear that may be present in individual therapy.

4. *Group therapy confronts adolescent narcissism.* So-called normal individuals are self-absorbed during adolescence. Troubled teens are even more likely to be focused on self, often to the exclusion of perspectives other than their own. The group has limited tolerance for such preoccupation. After all, peer members are themselves in need of the spotlight and are reluctant to share the stage with another for very long. The other group members tend to deal with the narcissistic one usually by being inattentive, sometimes by expressing disdain. This stance is usually enough to modify the behavior of the monopolizer. If not, it provides the therapist with considerable

support, making it easier to confront the narcissistic person in a more powerful yet less threatening manner than is available in individual therapy.

5. *Group therapy gives the teen a place to practice new social skills.* The group setting is both classroom and practice field for teens learning new social skills. The therapist's role as instructor of these skills is limited in individual therapy, where the therapist must depend on his or her own relationship with the adolescent and on the young person's reported experiences with others. In the group, the therapist can observe these peer interactions as they occur and intervene immediately if necessary.

Techniques such as how to enter into group discussions appropriately, how to assert one's self among others, and how to manage boredom, anger, or sadness in the group context are practiced. Standard rules of polite interaction also are explored. More abstract social skills, such as expression of empathy, respect, and concern for others, also may be acquired in the group experience.

6. *Group therapy provides an arena for building the ego strength of the group members.* Peer acceptance is a consuming concern for adolescents, and the bonding that can occur among group members in a therapy group may be a teenager's first experience of peer acceptance. This bonding, or group cohesiveness, does not occur accidentally. It depends on the group leader as surely as the music of an orchestra depends on the conductor. The experience of feeling accepted by peers is far and away a more powerful one than the acceptance of the therapist alone. As one adolescent put it, "Of course you like me, you're my therapist; you have to!" The development of assertiveness enhances ego strength as well. What better way to acquire assertive skills than to observe and practice their use in a group of peers supervised by a knowledgeable adult?

7. *Group therapy often minimizes the friction between staff (therapist, teacher, nurse, psychologist, counselor, technician, or psychiatrist) and client (student or patient).* This statement rings truest in an inpatient setting, although it applies to outpatient work as well. It is most applicable to those in charge of the milieu, usually the nursing staff, classroom teachers, school counselors, and mental health technicians. Often, the demands of daily responsibilities prevent the staff from having conversations with teens they supervise that go beyond brief encounters focusing on rules and regulations. Within that context, conflict inevitably arises.

Group therapy provides a time and a place where staff and teens can sit down together and get to know each other from a different perspective. Mistrust of staff may be prevented or resolved in a small group setting with carefully structured group experiences.

FISH OR CUT BAIT:
WHY DO STRUCTURED GROUPS?

The use of structured groups has been critiqued and criticized. A variety of conclusions have been drawn, both favoring and opposing the use of structure in group therapy.

Several convincing arguments support the use of structured groups for adolescents:

1. Adolescents lack the sophistication that life experiences provide the adult. They are often self-conscious and ill at ease in new situations. They are comfortable, however, with structured group experiences, such as school, church, and team sports.
2. Adolescents need facts and information about life. They need education about abstract concepts, such as loss, self-esteem, relationships with the same and other sex, and so on. These important arenas may not all be explored if left to the whim of unstructured sessions.
3. Many therapists are inexperienced in group work and lack confidence as group facilitators. The structured format provides a framework that defines the direction of the hour. This structure eliminates concerns about how the weekly group time will be spent and allows the leader to focus on the internal dynamics of the group.

ONLY FOOLS RUSH IN:
COULD I USE THIS MANUAL FOR MY GROUP?

Group Exercises can be used with a wide variety of adolescent groups. I have used the exercises in the various groups in the following list with success. However, I'm sure there are other types of adolescent groups that could also use the manual with favorable results.

Inpatient Settings

Psychiatric Settings

Inpatient settings are ideal for doing effective group work. The greatest advantage is the safe environment that an inpatient setting offers. The therapist can "push the envelope" in such settings without fear of unsupervised fall-out after group time. For example, sometimes the group activity can elicit strong emotions of loss, sadness, and anger, emotions that may need to surface to be resolved but that could also trigger acting-out behaviors, such as running away, or other self-destructive behaviors.

Exercises may elicit the behavior that led to institutionalization in the first place. This can be very therapeutic in that the behavior can be contained and addressed on the spot.

The therapeutic milieu of a good adolescent treatment facility will promote a sense of community among the patients. Everyday issues of community living can be processed through material generated by the exercises.

Treatment facilities are ideal for eliciting issues with authority figures. The exercises in the manual provide a way for the leader (an authority figure) to model authority and positive caring in a give-and-take exchange. The leader becomes a source not only of information but also of interesting activities.

Substance Abuse Programs

Substance Abuse Programs

The manual is helpful in substance abuse treatment for all the reasons listed under "Psychiatry," plus a few more. Because emotional development in an adolescent with an addictive disorder tends to arrest at the time using chemicals began, these teens are developmentally behind others in their age group. Exercises in the manual direct thinking and conversation to arenas that are crucial to all adolescents: emotionality, family, identity, etc. It gives the addicted adolescent some catch-up time and education in areas other than chemical dependency. Of course, the "Living With Chemicals" section speaks to chemical dependency issues specifically.

Sexual Abuse Treatment

I have used the manual in inpatient settings where special groups were a part of the treatment regime. Certainly, survivors of sexual abuse would be one of those. I believe the group therapy approach, as an adjunct to individual therapy, is a must for survivors (adolescent or adult!). The myth of uniqueness (no one else has gone through, or understands, what I have. Worse yet, no one else is as "bad" as I am) is sometimes tough to break through, and nothing does that like a group of people who share the same past trauma. The manual allows the group to address their identity as survivors without forgetting the rest of their identity as teens. One pitfall of working with survivors is that the person begins to see his or her whole identity in terms of the abuse. One should remind the teen that the abuse need not be the defining event of their lives.

(Note: I have not done Eating Disorder groups, but it seems the same would apply to teens with eating disorders in inpatient settings.)

Community Settings

Public Schools

The adolescent group work I have felt most passionate about is the work I have done in public schools. The school setting is the best place to identify teens at risk. It is also the best setting for prevention and intervention. If the public school is truly an advocate for the adolescents it serves, identification of and intervention for kids at risk should be a service provided within the system. School counselors should be facilitating groups for the high-risk students in their case loads.

High-risk teens bubble to the surface at school. Poor or dropping grades, problems with authority figures, marked absence from school, fighting with peers, sexual acting out, evidence of alcohol or drug use, and antisocial behavior of all kinds illuminate the at-risk adolescent. The school nurse, classroom teacher, and coach are excellent referral sources for kids at risk. Maintenance personnel and bus drivers are also good sources for information about high-risk students. Hopefully, there is a group program in place right in the school setting.

I have used the manual for "Between Teens Group" at a number of high schools. School staff referred students to the counseling office, where the counselors screened and evaluated each student in terms of his or her ability and willingness to participate in group. Groups met once a week during school hours.

Meeting during school hours is the most desirable but also the most difficult arrangement. Often, the counselor must convince administration and teachers that participation in group may be essential. The student may have to miss class on occasion, a consequence that seems minimal if the probability of dropping out or flunking out of school is high.

The method I have used with success is to assign group time on a rotating basis so that students do not miss the same class consistently. For example, on Week 1, Teen Group meets first hour on Monday; Week 2, second hour Tuesday; Week 3, third hour Wednesday, and so on.

I have also been in situations where the whole school has a study-hall-type hour at the same time every day. This presented an ideal time to schedule Teen Group.

The issue of parental approval must also be addressed. I have done groups in schools where the principal required specific permission forms be signed by parents. In other schools, the principal has waived any notification to parents, feeling the very kids who needed the group most would be those whose parents either wouldn't sign or would never get around to signing. Of course, the safest bet is to require parental approval in writing. Actually, I have not experienced any problems getting that. The language used to describe a Between Teens Group to parents is important. I have not experienced parental objection when flyers, brochures, or forms requesting parental approval focus on "increasing self-esteem" as the primary goal of the group experience.

Adolescents are a captive audience in their school setting. It is an ideal arena for identifying high-risk teens. When identification and intervention are possible in schools, and the professional staff is there, I don't understand why all schools don't have a group program for their students at risk.

Gay-Lesbian-Bisexual Centers

Although I have not facilitated adolescent groups in a lesbigay community center myself, this curriculum has been used successfully by others in such settings.

Studies have shown that the use of cocaine and other drugs is higher among lesbigay youth and that the suicide rate of lesbigay adolescents is higher than in heterosexual teens. One doesn't need studies to imagine that many adolescent issues (such as family support and peer acceptance) are complicated by lesbigay identity. A supportive, nonjudgmental group that meets on a regular basis is a loving way for the community to respond to the reality of homosexuality among teens.

Court-Ordered Programs

Drug and Alcohol Education Programs. I have used the manual in court-ordered alcohol and drug education programs for juvenile offenders. The exercises were a terrific way to make the educational requirements, tedious and boring when presented

teens adjudicated to such programs often have a number of problems contributing to the abuse.

Family Education Programs for Divorcing Couples. Many states require divorcing couples and their children to attend education programs. The family/domestic court may contract with particular providers for such services or allow participants to choose from a variety of sanctioned vendors. Parents are assigned to their own groups, children to groups according to age, and adolescents/teens to a group of their peers. The exercises in the manual provide a ready-made program. The group facilitator can select exercises that elicit the most desired material for discussion. For example, the exercise on perspective ("A Matter of Perspective") opens the door for discussion of the parents' differing perspectives on their divorce.

Church or Religious Education. I have used exercises in the manual for Christian education (Sunday school) with teens, on religious retreats, and as a part of conferences. I believe the manual could be used by those from other faith traditions with equal success.

The Private Sector

I have had only some success with adolescent groups in the private sector. My experience has been that getting the group together is a grisly task. In the midsized, midwestern city in which I live, there are not that many adolescents in therapy in the private sector. Those that are, are often from families that do not want to "air the family laundry"; therefore, they are not comfortable placing their troubled teens in a group. I hope this is not the case where you live.

When I did adolescent groups in my private practice, I did them in 8-week segments, one session per week. The groups, once off the ground, did as well as any.

NOTE: When doing groups, always require payment in full, up front.

I'm sure there are many wonderful marketing techniques for teen groups in private practice. You or your group or clinic could probably put a whiz-bang package together. Just know that the marketing is very important. Once you've got critical mass (I wouldn't do one without six members; you can count on at least one being absent at every session) you will *kiss* the manual because your work is practically done! In addition, I have not done outpatient groups with adolescents without a cotherapist. Just not that brave! (See "A Case for Cotherapy," pp. 29-30.)

FACT OR FANTASY

Experts in the field of adolescent group psychotherapy agree about several conditions that make for ideal group work. Like most fantasies, these ideas do not translate into reality for most of us, but they are useful aims.

1. *Selection of group members should be a careful process conducted by the group leader.* Ideally, the therapist arranges pregroup interviews with prospective members and chooses those who would benefit by the group experience or be an asset to the group (or both). Equally important is a conversation with new members about group therapy—what it is, why it is important, what can be expected in the sessions, and what behaviors are expected of group members.

More often than not, group therapists have no choice over group membership. Patients, clients, or students are assigned to your group in accordance with the policy of the institution or agency. Either group therapy is part of the program required by the facility for everyone, or group members are assigned due to the nature of their problem: for example, Special Issues Group (for sexually abused girls), CD Group (for chemically dependent teens), or Up and Over Group (for children of divorce).

Therapists working in large outpatient programs probably have the greatest freedom to choose their group members.

In the school setting, counselors may be able to choose group members from their case loads. This works best when the case load is small enough for the counselors to have at least some relationship with every student assigned to them. In situations where case loads are large, classroom teachers may be the best ones to refer students to their counselors for participation in Teen Group.

2. *Young adolescents work better in same-sex groups, whereas older teens generally fare best in mixed-sex groups.* Adolescents aged 11 to 13 are impulsive and distractible enough; mixing sexes is like peppering the chili. Same-sex groups are more likely to reflect the reality of their lives at this time. Heterosexual teens usually have a great deal of curiosity about members of the other sex, but girls tend to talk to other girls about the boys they like best, and boys usually evaluate girls from a distance. When mixed-sex relationships do exist, they often are managed partly within same-sex peer groups. Groups of boys meet groups of girls at local hangouts and pair off temporarily. Even determining who pairs with whom usually is choreographed and performed by same-sex friends, involving complicated rituals including exchanges by notes or messengers.

Older teens benefit by mixed-sex groups. By age 14 or 15, their attention is riveted to cross-sex concerns (assuming heterosexuality). Girls wonder how they are perceived by boys, and boys unceasingly monitor signs of acceptance or rejection from girls. Misconceptions about what the other sex really wants abound. Fear and frustration, expectation and anticipation shade boy-girl interactions during adolescence. The therapy group is an ideal arena for exploring nuances of gender.

3. *Group size should be 6 to 12 members.* "When two or three are gathered together . . . " only works in church. On the one hand, a group of two or three adolescents does not make for a dynamic group experience. On the other hand, in a group of 15, the stew is overwhelmed by the ingredients.

Often, the therapist does not have control over the number of members in his or her group. Census fluctuations in hospitals and agencies, lack of compliance in outpatient settings, or just the weather can cause group size to vary dramatically from week to week.

If only three people show up for a session, it is not a group, so do something special. Take them someplace different; to the park or to the snack bar or the cafeteria. Offer to let them pick the topic for the hour. Tell them you are excited to have this opportunity to get to know them better because the group is now so small.

If your group explodes from 8 to 20 and your group room holds 12, split the group into two, and have a separate session with each smaller group. Another option is to keep the group together and use one of the exercises in the curriculum that works well for a large group—for example, "Boy-Girl Relationships" or "Breaking the Ice." Find a larger room to use, if you can; teenagers love to be in a new or different environment (especially if they are institutionalized).

4. *Therapy groups should have closed membership once the group has begun, and the life of the group should be known to members from the start.* The life of a group should be predetermined and announced. For example, "Between Teens Group will meet on Wednesday nights from 7 to 9 p.m., August 5 through September 9."

Closed membership provides the best arena for the evolution of group process because participants can become acquainted without the distraction and disruption of sudden comings and goings of fellow group members. Reality often deals the therapist a different hand: Group membership changes in accordance with the admission and discharge activities of the institution. Although outpatient work may be less susceptible to changing membership, family or school requirements may cause missed sessions and group members may drop out, causing group composition to vary.

This manual is addressed to the changing nature of adolescent group membership by providing self-contained exercises; that is, each group session is in and of itself a complete experience. The group will move through the usual stages of forming, storming, and norming in each session, but at a much greater speed. Also, within a session, the stages will be less distinctly defined.

If your groups can be arranged so that membership is closed, so much the better. The activities of the curriculum provide a foundation on which group development can build. If, however, your groups must have the flexibility of open membership, the curriculum will be helpful. No doors are left open or agendas left hanging when each group session ends.

THE GOOD NEWS

The good news is that despite less-than-ideal conditions, your group probably will work anyway. There is no substitute for a leader's confidence, enthusiasm, and optimism in the face of adversity. It takes a creative spirit to manage five squirming 11- and 12-year-olds in a group with two sophisticated 17-year-olds. Only a leader who is a good sport can cope when a great-looking 16-year-old male is ushered into the group with the "terrible trio"—three giggly, boy-crazed 14-year-old females. The ability to turn these obstacles into opportunities lies in the skill and attitude of the group leader. The structure of a predetermined plan for each group session can be an anchor for the therapist in unsettling conditions. The group with the giggly girls may need to talk about the trio, especially if the gigglers are powerful and distracting. Use the heightened emotionality created by the new boy's arrival in the group to examine the impact of the trio on the whole group. Elicit responses from other members but set a gently supportive tone for the confrontation yourself.

At other times, a group may sail too far off course, loose bearings altogether, and head for dangerous waters (or get stuck in deadly calm, which can be equally hazardous). The facilitator can intervene by changing the direction with a planned exercise and alter the course.

The leader can use the curriculum like a captain navigates a ship. The destination of the journey is determined, and the course charted. What happens along the way is influenced by the weather and the spirit of the crew.

GRIST FOR THE MILL

In group therapy, as in individual therapy, almost anything is grist for the mill. If your group does not respond well to one of the exercises, do not plow on through and pretend you don't notice. Comment on how apathetic or preoccupied or downright rebellious the group is and ask what's going on. Sometimes, they just may not like the exercise; at other times, it might mean the group has hidden agendas you do not know about, such as Becky broke up with Daniel. Sometimes, it is an event outside the group. I remember a case in which the most popular boy in the patient community was being discharged. He was not a member of the group I was leading, but most of the group was in semiofficial mourning over the loss of Mr. Wonderful. Fine, talk about these things. Remember that a structured exercise is a diving board into deeper waters. You do not need it if your group has already taken the plunge.

Unexpected reactions generated by the exercises should be processed. Sexual abuse issues bubble up at surprising times. I once had a girl in my group who was sculpting her family ("Family Sculpting" exercise) and burst into tears when she positioned her uncle. When I asked about her tears, she revealed that this uncle had sexually abused her. This kind of incident merits attention from the therapist and the group. It needs to take precedence over the exercise for awhile; however, it should not be allowed to become the focus of the hour. It was important that this girl be supported in her decision to reveal the situation to the group. However, she also needed the leader to intervene and protect her from overexposing herself to a group of young people who were not able to handle much material of this nature. It is a difficult balancing act for the therapist. One needs to allow expression of difficult material so that members will not feel that their situation is too awful to be discussed and also to protect them from overexposing themselves.

Sometimes, teenagers will overexpose themselves despite the leader's diligence. You may or may not know when this occurs. For example, during the "T-Shirts" exercise, a group member drew satanic images and symbols on the back of his T-shirt worksheet. As processing began, the boy tore up his worksheet. When this behavior was questioned by the leader, the boy angrily retorted that the exercise was stupid. Actually, he realized he had revealed too much and so destroyed the evidence. However, a clue had been observed that played an important role in subsequent therapy. Another time, a tough-girl type revealed a source of pain and humiliation by talking about an incident in which she felt abandoned by her mother. When she was that honest and vulnerable in group, she blew her cover (as tough and uncaring) and exposed her more sensitive side. Her reaction was to act out to such a point that she had to be asked to leave the session. This was a time when processing the event during group was inappropriate. It had to be done one-on-one with the group leader after the session. She was not ready to expose her pain to the group, and when she accidentally did, she grabbed for the "covers" (by acting out) to hide her emotional nakedness.

A member's misbehavior during a session can be a basis for valuable discussion. If the leader can enlist peers to confront the deviant, so much the better. Just remember not to allow too much attention to be focused on one teen for too long; that attention can become a secondary gain and encourage, rather than discourage, acting out in the future.

Conflict between members or between leader and member also can be grist for the mill. It is usually appropriate and important to bring any actual or perceived conflict to the light of the discussion, even if it means stopping the group process to do so. If the issue is between you, as the leader, and a member, work through it right then and there. You can model conflict resolution for the entire group, not to mention the positive impact on the member involved when you resolve the problem.

Also be sure to discuss the situation with the group when you ask a member to leave or have a member removed from a session.

THE DANCE OF DISCIPLINE

Between Teens Group should be a place where teens feel free to express themselves. However, the importance of structure and limits cannot be overemphasized. These two conditions seem mutually exclusive, but they really are not.

Most institutional settings, including treatment facilities and schools, have fairly rigid behavior codes that can be relaxed during group. Between Teens Group should not feel like a class. Although instruction and learning occur in group, these are not the primary objectives. Developing a sense of belonging and enhancing self-awareness and self-esteem are the goals of Between Teens Groups. Creating an atmosphere that promotes these objectives is one of the leader's greatest challenges. The leader must define and deliver discipline effectively. Reading the Group Statement at the beginning of each session is a good way to emphasize acceptable and unacceptable behavior. It defines the rules and reminds the group that orderly conduct is expected. When a group member (instead of the leader) reads the Group Statement, it tends to place the locus of control with the members. Actually, this placement is illusionary because the group is not in charge of disciplinary decisions or action; the leader is. However, the Group

Statement (p. 39) encourages ownership of the group, which is good: "This is our group. Its success or failure is up to us."

The group leader should maintain responsibility for all of the disciplinary activity for several reasons. The most obvious reason is that the number-one goal of Between Teens Group is to create a sense of belonging to a group. Peer-determined discipline would place group members in adversary roles. Even if the structure of your agency or institution is based on peer-determined discipline, it is not an advisable format for Between Teens Groups. Another reason is that many troubled teens have very few role models of responsible adult authority figures who are both supportive and able to confront. The group leader may be the only responsible adult with whom the teen connects—or one of a very few. A leader who models support, compassion, and acceptance with a fearless commitment to maintaining order is therapeutic. The possibility for corrective reparenting experiences exists in relationship with such an adult. This is not to say that peer confrontation is not desirable, because it is. Peer confrontation is a powerful therapeutic tool; however, responsibility for disciplinary action must fall to the group leader.

SPEAKING THE LANGUAGE

Cursing is not tolerated in the classroom or on the patient unit, but the use of four-letter expletives can be appropriate in the therapy group. This is true for both group members and therapist. If a member is working through an emotionally charged agenda and is reprimanded by the leader for inappropriate language, a potentially powerful therapeutic opportunity probably will be missed. By the time a troubled teen gets to group therapy, he or she already has been judged and condemned by adults. Connection with a nonjudgmental adult can be a healing factor, so allow teens to express themselves in the language they are comfortable with. If, however, it is obvious that members of the group are cursing simply for effect, the leader has the responsibility to confront and limit the overboard behavior.

It is equally powerful for the therapist to use expressions that would not be appropriate in other treatment settings. For example, if a teen's affect and attitude are the focus of the group and the therapist says, "I don't think you're all that burdened with guilt, I think you are mainly pissed off" and the interpretation is correct, an instantaneous connection is made between therapist and teen. Not only does the young person know that the leader understands but he or she also feels the freedom to respond in his or her own vernacular. It can be empowering to allow teens the freedom of expression during group time. It is also a good opportunity to emphasize the notion that there is a time and a place for everything. Cursing on occasion in group does not mean that the same behavior will not be punished outside the group. Remind your group that adults may curse in the stands at a baseball game, but they better not curse at a judge; they might be thrown in jail for it!

KEEPING THE PEACE

The Group Statement outlines two unacceptable behaviors: side conversations and unkindness. Unkind or disrespectful behavior between members or between members and therapist should not be tolerated. If this behavior already has been treated as grist for the mill and it surfaces again, it is time to take action.

The easiest, least messy approach is to kick the offender out of group. Troubled teens will act out in group just as they do everywhere else. They will test the limits to see how far they can go. When the limits are enforced, the members feel safe. It is important for teenagers to know that there is something bigger and stronger outside themselves. Enforcing group rules reassures them that you are in control. Remember that structure is like a safety net for adolescents: There is room for movement inside a net, but behavior is contained. The adult leading group therapy must carefully guide group process so that members feel his or her support and guidance and also feel the freedom to practice independent behavior.

Side conversations are always an issue in adolescent groups. Cliques and couples often identify themselves by sitting together and whispering and signaling one another. It is a way certain members will set themselves apart from the rest of the group. The unspoken message is a declaration of elitism and is counterproductive to group bonding. A simple 3-step procedure works well:

1. *Mention.* Remind the offending twosome (or threesome or whatever) that side conversations are not allowed in group.
2. *Move.* If the problem continues, separate the offenders by having them change places with other group members.
3. *Remove.* If they persist in communicating among themselves, kick them (or him or her, if there is only one instigator) out of the session. When you do that, you prioritize your commitment to the group over the individual or individuals. This action is also a wonderful way to confront the narcissistic notion that self is more important than other.

Always arrange before the next session a brief one-on-one exchange with whomever you kicked out of group. Invite the offender back and insist on a contract, verbal or written, that behavior will be appropriate. If a teen will not contract with you, express disappointment but respect his or her choice.

It goes without saying that group leaders must exercise great care in preserving the dignity of members at all times, especially during discipline. The need to reprimand or even remove a member from group does not imply the freedom to humiliate. It can be powerfully therapeutic to discipline with dignity.

HORSES OF A DIFFERENT COLOR:
DIFFICULT GROUP MEMBERS

Troubled teens are difficult by definition. This does not mean they will not be wonderful group members. Some, however, are problematic in groups. They usually fit into one of two profiles.

The Distracters

Distracters delight in disturbing, delaying, devaluing, demobilizing, defying, devastating, degrading, and debilitating group process. Frankly, you would like to kill them. The only thing that curtails your natural human inclination to retaliate in kind is the certain knowledge that these teens have good reasons for behaving as they do (that, and the fact that you do not want to be sued!).

Distracters often honeymoon in groups until they have surveyed the lay of the land. Their polite, compliant behavior makes you suspect someone has got this child all wrong. Then ka-blam! A shot is fired, the flag is raised, and the true colors are shown.

Distracters usually come to group therapy with a long history of acting-out behavior. Parents are miffed (or do not care), teachers have all but given up (if the teen is still in school), and other therapy attempts have not borne fruit. It is your turn. You may fail as well, but take heart; there is a silver lining to the stormy cloud. If a distracter cannot be shepherded into the flock, lessons still will be learned by all. For example, if a distracter is removed from the group—for one or two sessions or forever—the group can process this situation together. Ask several group members how they feel about the distracter's behavior. Tell the group how you feel about having to kick this person out. You can model the attitude of healthy parents and authority figures by being kind and accepting of the person while not accepting the inappropriate behavior.

STRESS

The confusion created when one's mind overrides the body's basic desire to choke the living daylights out of some kid who desperately deserves it.

You may be able to engage minor-league distracters in therapy by giving them the attention they seem to be asking for, but beat them to the punch. Single out a distracter. Ask him or her to read the Group Statement and let him or her have the "it" role in the exercise, if possible. Two purposes are served in this: One, you are giving a distracter the gifts of respect and your personal interest. Two, the other group members will see that you have given it your best shot.

If this procedure fails and acting out continues, you may be dealing with a real pro. It is time to pull out all the stops. The second line of defense is peer pressure. If you can enlist the aid of other group members in confronting the distracter, you may win the battle. Simply announce that you have done all you are willing to do for now and ask the group how they feel about a distracter. This is risky. Adolescents can be ruthless. It is hoped that you already have modeled compassionate confrontation, thereby setting the tone.

If a distracter is powerful and popular in the group, your challenge is greater. Sometimes, given enough rope, distracters will "hang" themselves. The group may grow weary of the distracters' antics, regardless of how clever they may be. Funny is only funny for so long. A distracter's negative attitude eventually loses its cool quotient. If it appears that the group is tiring or may tire in the near future, hang in there and continue to work with the distracter. Remember that peer pressure is a most powerful and therapeutic force; if the group will confront, it is your best bet. If that technique does not bring fairly quick results or if a distracter is such an obnoxious entity that you know the group would devour him or her if you gave them free rein to confront, you must take action. Kick the distracter out. It is a last resort, but it is often a winner. It establishes your control and demonstrates your concern for and commitment to the rest of the group.

If you must kick a distracter out, do so with a firm but empathic demeanor. Take care to treat him or her with respect. Then, when removal is arranged (by calling in a staff member, having your cotherapist remove him or her, phoning parents, or whatever), discuss with the group what just transpired. Do not take too long to process this or else you will end up with the same symptom you just treated—more distraction.

Last, meet with the distracter before the next group session. Your intent is to offer him or her one more chance. If you are met with defiance and a generally bad attitude, throw in the towel.

Some adolescents just will not do well in group work, or it may be that they are not ready for group therapy. It may become a possibility after some intensive individual therapy. It may be that they have not suffered the consequences of inappropriate behavior long enough. It could be that the root of the problem has not been identified or addressed. It is also possible that it is a developmental issue. Troubled teens sometimes do not mature like their better-adjusted peers. A 15-year-old with the social maturity of a 9-year-old will not do well in a Between Teens Group.

Many things can contribute to the acting-out behavior that makes an adolescent an unacceptable group member. The distracter and his or her parents deserve an explanation of his or her removal from the group. As always, the truth, couched in compassionate rhetoric, and a recommendation for the next course of action is your strong suit.

The Attractor

Attractors are the anxious, afraid, apathetic, inarticulate, awkward teens who pull attention to themselves like a magnet. Through the personification of passivity and needs crying out to be met, a subtle power emanates from these quiet ones in the group.

Initially, attractors elicit caretaking behavior from other group members. This may mean that other members try to draw out the quiet ones by solicitous inquiry or encouragement. Or it could be just the opposite: Group members may avoid any attempt at interacting with attractors, thereby aligning with their conspiracy of silence. Often, other group members become defenders of the withdrawn posture of attractors.

The group may come down hard on the leader who breaks the unspoken rule not to tamper with these fragile vessels. It is as if the group is determined to protect these conscientious objectors. Be prepared for some hostility from the group when you intervene (as you must) to confront an attractor. You may be attempting to draw him or her into the group discussion or activity or you may be illuminating group process by exposing the power of this quiet one. If the group reacts to your intervention, use the reaction to underscore the caretaking response elicited by the attractors. This is the perfect opportunity to focus on other members instead of becoming "attracted" to the quiet one. Tease out the reaction and responses of the members who rushed to the defense of the attractor, and explore that with them.

Attractors and distracters have a lot in common. They disrupt group process by their respective behaviors, and both command the group's attention sooner or later. Although a distracter captures attention by stirring the pot, an attractor captures attention by presenting an irresistible force. An attractor is to the group what the light bulb is to the moth.

An attractor may be a frightened, damaged child in need of the most sensitive and careful approach, or an attractor may be the most defiant rebel in the group. It is crucial that the facilitator assess the character of an attractor quickly because very different approaches are required.

Sometimes, an attractor is transformed into a working group member right before your eyes. If this person seems the quiet rebel, refusing to participate in the group as an act of defiance, announce it to the group with a good deal of bemused respect. Applaud the skill exhibited in rebelling in this powerful manner. You may luck out and surprise the socks off a teen who is convinced that adults are both blind and stupid. Your expressed respect for this chosen position will both flatter an attractor and deflate his or her resistance. This technique is not always an instant success, but it often works, and therefore it is worth a try.

The truly miserably shy and insecure adolescent may benefit the most from a group experience. Nothing speaks as loudly as peer group acceptance. If you can facilitate expressions of genuine kindness and concern for the worth of an attractor, even the shyest and most withdrawn teen can metamorphose into an animated, productive group member. This transformation may be easier said than done, depending on the health of the rest of the group. If collective pathologies are such that group bonding is nearly impossible, you might not be able to hope that the group can be an effective support system for the attractor. In that case, beware! Your natural inclination may be to rush in and become an attractor's defender. This action will only further alienate him or her from the group. Another temptation is to catch this wounded one for a little one-on-one interaction after the group session. Then, in conspiratorial fashion, you can explain how messed up the rest of the group is, how so-and-so and so-and-so have so many problems themselves, that they are not able to reach out to anyone, and so forth. In other words, you find yourself explaining away the behavior of the other group members. Big mistake. This tactic only distances attractors from other members even more and does not allow them to learn to deal with the harsh realities of rejection in all of its unpleasant forms.

A much more productive and empowering move is to do all of this work in the group hour. Talk about how you, as the leader, feel about how the group is treating the attractor. Remind the group that it is against the rules to be unkind to anyone in the group (see the Group Statement). If you can, enlist the group in a discussion about this rule; if you cannot, simply enforce the rule. Usually, the mention of the rule is enough. In extreme cases, when members continue to pick at an attractor (who by now is entrenched firmly in the role of scapegoat), terminate the session. This may be hard to do in outpatient settings. In inpatient settings, send the patients back to their rooms for the remainder of the group hour.

Like distracters, attractors will not change their behavior as long as there is a payoff. If nonparticipation elicits attention—either in caretaking behavior from other group members or in maligned barbs and innuendo—and attention is the payoff, the behavior will continue.

A CASE FOR COTHERAPY

Although a cotherapist is not always essential when working with adolescent groups, having one offers a number of benefits. There is something to be said for a show of force, and two adult leaders in a group of six to eight teens help emphasize the power base. It is nice to have the assistance of a cotherapist when kicking a disruptive group member out of a session. The cotherapist can escort the teen to an appropriate place— for example, back to his or her room, to the lobby to await transportation home, or to the principal's office. A cotherapist of the other sex re-creates the mother-father dynamic, which enhances the possibility of corrective reparenting experiences in the group. A cotherapist is essential when the group facilitator is a consultant from outside the institution or agency. In this case, the cotherapist is a liaison between the group and the facility staff.

A cotherapist may be protection for the group leader both physically and legally. If a threat of physical violence is inherent in your group, which may be due to the population your group members come from or because of events outside your group (e.g., chaos and conflict on the unit), a cotherapist is needed. Likewise, one should consider the benefit of a cotherapist in case a member or members of a group attempt to misrepresent group proceedings. It is a chilling experience to learn that group members are telling others that the leader said or did this or that and it is not true! If your facility does not have the budget or personnel to supply a cotherapist, or if you prefer working alone, consider audiotaping your sessions for your own protection.

THE KEYS TO SUCCESS

Between Teens Groups are successful if something happens for individual members. It may happen when a member realizes he or she likes group because he or she feels a real part of a group of peers. It may happen through an "aha!" experience when a member identifies a loss and finds himself or herself in the loss cycle. It might be when one peer observes obnoxious behavior in another and recognizes himself or herself. It could be when one member is confronted by another in a truly compassionate manner.

The group therapist cannot make things happen, as a gardener cannot make things grow. The gardener prepares the soil, plants the seeds, pulls the weeds, prays for rain, and waters if necessary. Likewise, the group leader creates the best environment possible; seeds and teens grow on their own.

The single most important condition necessary for successful group therapy with adolescents is the therapist's attitude. Knowledge and technique are important, but attitude is everything.

Attitude is informed by the therapist's commitment to the basic conditions of the therapeutic relationship. These conditions were identified by Carl Rogers (1961) and are discussed here as they apply to group work with teens:

1. Contact

Each member of your group must feel some personal contact with you. Making contact is more an art than a science. There are a million ways to make contact. Teens are extremely sensitive to adults in authority. They can discern disinterest in a heart-beat. Your recognition of each group member as an individual is essential; making contact is the unspoken "*I see you*" that must be said. It may mean a one-on-one conference with each group member prior to his or her joining your group (the ideal); it may mean selecting a member for a special role in a group activity; and it may mean your correct interpretation of a teen's emotion or belief during a session.

2. Congruence

You, as leader, must be who you say you are. If you encourage self-disclosure as a part of emotional healing but then judge and criticize material that is shared, your group will condemn you as a phony. If you talk about the equality of all people but then give preferential treatment to the girls in your group over the boys, your credibility is shattered. If you are angry with a member of the group and pretend you are not, the group will know. If you find yourself favoring and protecting a certain group member or avoiding and cutting off another, you had better talk about it with your group. Owning your prejudices and inconsistencies reinstates your authenticity.

3. Positive Regard

Valuing each group member is a must; that does not mean it comes easily or naturally. The behavior of troubled teens can give the word *obnoxious* a whole new meaning. The therapist working with a group of these individuals often must do conscious mental gymnastics to maintain positive regard. This may mean using self-talk techniques with yourself, such as: "This teen is not a warrior, this teen is wounded" or "This teen has to be in love with himself because no one else is" or "This teen acts out because she was acted on" or "This teen pretends to be fearless because he is so full of fear." It is usually possible to ferret out the pain that drives the behavior. It is the best way I know to preserve the respect one must have for each member of a group.

4. Empathy

If contact says, "I see you," empathy says, "I understand you." The ability to be with a teen in whatever struggle or discovery he or she encounters in group is both supportive and empowering.

Adolescents often do not understand themselves. Identifying and naming feeling states is foreign territory. Helping them understand their emotions is powerful. Interpretation is a more effective tool for therapists working with adolescents than for therapists working with adults. It may be painfully obvious to you that Jimmy is sad about his mother's remarriage; Jimmy, however, may not be in touch with that at all. He acts angry and says he is "confused." If you gently suggest that maybe he feels very sad about losing his mother to some other guy, and if you are right, a profound release and relief is experienced by Jimmy. He realizes, "Yes, that's it!" and understands himself. He also knows that you understand him.

5. Perception

You may be the world's warmest, most compassionate, empathic group therapist, but if your group does not feel it, it will not matter. Group members must perceive your contact, congruence, positive regard, and empathy. The expression of these qualities is as varied as the individuals leading groups. The use of humor, expressions of approval and affection, methods of confrontation, and tolerance limits are but a few of the channels through which messages are sent by the group leader to his or her group. I hope you are working with adolescents because you love to. Their energy, innocence, and even their insolence captivate and motivate you to be your best self. If this mysterious affection for your clients drives your work, your group will perceive it.

The material just listed, and that to follow, is (or should be) basic for all therapists. It is included here for two reasons: One, even the most sophisticated therapist can lose sight of these conditions; they are forgotten due to burnout, discounted through a commitment to some newer and mightier therapeutic construct, or simply lost in one's repertoire of approaches. Two, in reality, group therapy often is facilitated by wonderful, well-intentioned leaders who have precious little formal education in the therapy business. I hope this overview of the therapeutic relationship will serve as a refresher for some and a fresh start for others.

Techniques inherent in the therapeutic relationship are equally valid in the group context (again, from the work of Carl Rogers, 1961).

1. Adoption of a Nonjudgmental Attitude

A nonjudgmental attitude is a must for therapists of adolescents and should not interfere with the therapist's responsibility to model a sound and acceptable value system. In other words, the therapist can model, in behavior and verbal expression, respect for authority, environment, and individual without condemning a group member who does not appear to value these things.

2. Listening

Every member of your group has the need and the right to be heard. The leader's attentiveness to each group member is crucial. When you, as leader, have difficulty listening to one of your members, you can bet that everyone else does too. Use this problem as a therapeutic opportunity. Talk to that teen, right in group, about how hard it is for you to listen to him or her. Emphasize how important it is that you and the group hear what needs to be heard from that individual. Then discuss the problem, whatever it is—rambling on and on and taking forever to make a point, talking too softly, always changing the subject, an angry sarcastic affect, or whatever. It is important that your group know you listen to them all.

3. Expressing Acceptance

Acceptance is the balm that heals many wounds. Often, change comes only through acceptance. If you can accept your group members right where they are, they have very little reason to struggle against you.

4. Self-Disclosing

The gentle art of self-disclosing may be the trickiest of them all. Adolescents need to know you as a real person, but adult-child boundaries must be clear. It is about being with them without becoming one of them.

I remember an experience from my early days as a group therapist. I was exasperated and nearly defeated by a boy in my group who defiantly refused to self-disclose on any level. Feeling desperate, I finally told him that if he would share something of himself with the group, he could ask me something about myself. Without hesitation or batting an eye, he spoke at last about events precipitating his hospital admission. Then, with a smug look, he asked me how many times a week I had sex. Be careful.

WALKING THE TIGHTROPE

It is a challenge for the group therapist to maintain balance between validation and confrontation. An atmosphere of acceptance and support promotes a sense of belonging to the group. The use of confrontation, however, especially peer confrontation, is a powerful and effective tool for change. Supporting and validating group members while encouraging constructive confrontation takes concentration and a sense of purpose on the leader's part.

The Three R's Plus One

I talk to the parents of teens about the four R's of parenting adolescents. Group leaders of adolescents can follow the same formula:

1. *Rules.* Set reasonable rules for your group and enforce them.
2. *Relevance.* Understand the adolescent culture. Speak the language, be familiar with the ever-changing trends and customs, and know the music and dress code. Teens do not trust adults in the first place; do not widen the gap with lack of savvy about their world.
3. *Reward.* Do not forget to reward positive behavior and attitude. It often means making a conscious effort to look for it. It is easy to fall into the habit of watchdogging for bad behavior, especially in an inpatient facility where rules and regulations are intricately tied to treatment. Train yourself to be alert for the smallest signs of success; then, reward the teen (or the group) with praise.
4. *Respect.* The importance of adults treating adolescents with respect was underscored for me one year when I addressed the adolescent participants of a state PTA conference. The organizers of the event told me I would be speaking to teenagers. I assumed it would be high school students. Imagine my surprise when I discovered that about 70% of the audience were translescents—12 to 14 years old! My topic was, "Everything You Wanted to Know About Relationships But Were Afraid To Ask"; when I saw this collection of mostly very young teens, I freaked! I did the gig as planned (I was to speak for an hour and a half—too long for that age group). The audience lasted about 45 minutes, then became a squirming mass of humanity.

   At the end of the presentation, all of the participants filled out evaluation forms. I knew I was dead in the water! Expecting the worst, I was shocked to find I got very positive responses. The young participants thanked me for treating them like they knew something. My presentation, geared to 16-year-olds and 17-year-olds, made these younger kids feel respected. It was a good lesson.

As therapists, we all work from some basic philosophy. The following list outlines a compassionate, responsible approach to mental health care:

A Philosophy for the Therapist

A. A person is basically good. "No one sets out to be bad."

B. All behavior is purposeful. This means that each person is "doing the best he or she can" to meet his or her needs at this time.

C. A person can learn a better way to meet personal needs.

D. A person needs to be able to make choices even in a setting that limits freedom.

E. A person will not change if there is nothing in it for him or her.

F. By changing behavior, a person can change thinking and attitudes.

G. By changing thinking and attitudes, a person can change behavior.

H. An environment that reinforces positive behavior facilitates change more than one that focuses on negative behavior.

YOU'RE OFF AND RUNNING, BUT IF YOU STUMBLE . . .

Working with adolescent groups is more like hiking a wilderness trail than following a beaten path. Roadblocks and pitfalls are part of the natural terrain. I hope this travel guide will inform and reassure the novice or the expert. The following are common bumps on the trail:

1. *Your group is completely apathetic, nonverbal, and appears bored out of their collective gourd.* Apathy may be the most fearsome foe faced by the adolescent group therapist. Teenagers are accustomed to being entertained. Television, movies, videos, sophisticated audio systems, and computer games are hard acts to follow. You may need to talk about that. Verbalize the obvious—that the group seems less than enthusiastic about therapy. Remind them of the Group Statement: "This is our group. Its success or failure is up to us." See whether you can develop interaction about the almost tangible apathy (the grist for the mill approach). Sometimes, an entire session will develop out of discussing what is wrong, and you can scrap the exercise planned. Sometimes, a group needs to have an unstructured session to just kick back and let agendas surface naturally. If you sense this situation, check it out with your group. If they concur, great; if it falls on unresponsive ears, tell your group to hang in there with you and to trust the process. Then go on with the exercise. The exercises in this manual were selected because they were received favorably by a large number of adolescents. Usually, the exercise itself will pull your group out of the hole of apathy. Trust it.

2. *The group is chaotic, disruptive, and attentive to any agenda but the scheduled one.* On occasion, the collective chemistry of a group is combustible due to the mix of individuals. More often, events outside the group combine to whip the atmosphere to gale force. The first line of defense is a stern, businesslike approach. This attitude may be enough, especially if your usual demeanor is laid-back and relaxed. However, it may be like pissing in the wind. If so, it is time for the Big Gun; you had better have one.

Dismissing one member from a group session is a good way to gain control over the others. Boot out more than one only if there is no other way. When two go out together, it is much less embarrassing, and the risk goes up that the group will glorify the rascals as heroes.

3. *The group is not supportive, nurturing, or even attentive to one another.* Go for dramatic effect in this one. Stop the session cold. Stand up. Walk around the group circle and lecture your head off about the dismal lack of group regard for one another, about the pathetic self-focus and selfishness that dominates attitude and behavior, about the incredible lack of the most basic social skills or awareness. Then end the session and send them all packing. This technique works best in an inpatient setting where the adolescents can be sent to their rooms. If this is not possible, be creative. Make them stay in the group room and *you* leave. Let your cotherapist or other staff guard the errant group Gestapo style. No talking, no moving, and so on. This response to a very nonempathic group makes two points: One, lack of regard for one another is totally unacceptable; two, there are worse ways to spend the group hour.

4. *The group seems to have their own agenda, and it isn't yours.* Unless there is a clear reason not to, go with the group's agenda. Remember that the purpose of a structured exercise is to create an agenda. If the group has one, there is no need to reinvent the wheel.

5. *The therapist says or does the wrong thing.* This bump is hard for the therapist but good for the group. It provides a real-life situation in which the therapist can model healthy behavior.

This hazard has played out for me in a number of situations; most often, I go too far with my confrontational style and hurt someone's feelings. Sometimes, I am misinterpreted, and a group member gets hurt or angry. When you become aware that something is amiss, check it out. Point out the clue—a red face, sudden withdrawal from interaction, an obvious change in sitting position or posture, tears, a change in expression—and ask about it: "Diego, I noticed when I said that, that your whole expression changed. What's going on?" or "Diego, did I hurt your feelings a minute ago?" or "Diego, I think I just pushed too hard, didn't I?" Identify what happened, exchange perceptions with the member, own your part, and apologize if necessary. If you are unclear about an interaction, ask the group: "Diego is saying nothing is wrong here. Did anyone else notice Diego's reaction to what I said as unusual, or was it just me?" or "Does anyone else think Diego looks hurt, or is it just me?" or "Do you (group members) think I was a little too rough on Diego?" It can be very empowering for the group if they unite against you now and then. It can be very empowering for the individual member if the group agrees with his or her perspective instead of yours. Always own your mistakes, always apologize. It is what we want from them.

6. *A group member says or does the wrong thing.* This pitfall ranges from what is said to what is done. Maybe one member says something hurtful to another; maybe a teen is blatantly rude to the therapist or cotherapist. Maybe a group member crawls under the furniture during a session or injures another member during an exercise. That has

happened to me. During a "Trust Walk" exercise, one young adolescent, just being playful, walked his "blind" partner right into a wall. The resulting injury required a trip to the emergency room and six sutures. We spent the remainder of that session, and most of the next one, talking about what it is like to do something that results in pain for someone else. Always be alert to opportunities for processing the here and now. In the case of the "Trust Walk" exercise injury, the whole group felt involved in what happened. This group was hospitalized in a treatment program and all had caused pain and disappointment to others. The accident became a marvelous vehicle through which the greater significance of their hospitalization could be explored.

If a member says something rude or sarcastic to you, a therapeutic opportunity is right around the corner. Confront the teen about his or her remark or behavior and then ask whose face you have on: As an adult authority figure, are you Mom? Dad? Teacher (which one)? A grandparent? After exploring that, share your perspective with the teen. Tell him or her how it makes you feel when a young person is sarcastic and rude. I don't know about you, but I want to retaliate—get 'em back, put 'em in their place, show 'em who's really boss! Usually, an adult authority figure can do just that to an adolescent. Sometimes, adolescents will rethink their behavior when they realize it is costly to them. Although you cannot allow insolent behavior to go unchecked, it can expose a therapeutic window.

PART

3

THE CURRICULUM

The Group Statement

This is our group. Its success or failure is up to us. We come together in search of ourselves. What we have to share is honesty; what we hope to gain is trust. Through expressing our feelings, hopes, and dreams, we can become known to one another. Friendship and self-understanding are the rewards. We will respect the privacy of each member by keeping group business within the group. What we see here, what we say here, what we hear here, let it stay here.

There are only two rules for this group: (a) No side conversations are allowed, and (b) we must be kind to one another.

BREAKING THE ICE

OBJECTIVES

I. Behavioral

Members will

1. Speak up in the group by responding to direct questions
2. Self-disclose by answering direct questions

II. Cognitive

Members will

1. Enhance development of group identity by exchanging personal information in a structured format
2. Increase awareness of self and others by exchanging feedback

MATERIALS

"Breaking the Ice: Group Leader Instructions" (p. 45)

METHOD

Questions are read by the group leader. Each member responds to each question.

INSTRUCTIONS

Read "Breaking the Ice: Group Leader Instructions" aloud to the group. Follow the format outlined.

CONCLUSION

The final eight questions do a good job of pulling the focus of the group to the here and now. No additional wrap-up is needed.

AUTHOR'S COMMENT

This exercise is a good one for a newly formed group or a group with an influx of new members. I also like to use it to slow the pace of a group that has had several intense sessions—it's a nice breather.

BREAKING THE ICE:
GROUP LEADER INSTRUCTIONS

> *NOTE:* This section may be read to the group as written or be explained in the leader's own words:

This exercise will help us learn more about one another. If we are strangers now, we won't be at the end of the exercise. If we know each other well now, we'll probably learn something new about one another.

I will ask a question. Each group member will answer the question one at a time around the circle. Everyone must answer every question; however, you may "pass" if you need some time to think, and I'll come back to you.

Listen closely to each person's response. Each member of this group is a unique and important individual.

Questions

1. What is the best movie you've ever seen?
2. Who is the most important person to have lived during your lifetime?
3. If you could be an animal other than a human, what would you be, and why?
4. What was the best day of your life?
5. What is your earliest memory?
6. What is your biggest worry?
7. What would you like to be doing 5 years from now?
8. If you had $5,000, what would you do with it?
9. What is one thing you *don't* like about being in this group? What is one thing you *do* like about being in this group?
10. One of the things people like most about me is . . . One of the things people like least about me is . . .
11. My favorite performer/entertainer is . . .
12. The season I like best is . . . Why?
13. The person in this group who has the most trouble sharing himself or herself with others is . . .
14. The person I learned most about today is . . .
15. The person in this group who is *most* like me is . . . The person in this group who is *least* like me is . . .
16. The person in this group with whom I could spend the longest time on a desert island is . . . Why?
17. The person in this group who enjoys life the most is . . .
18. The person in this group whom I would like to know more about is . . .
19. The person in this group who scares me a little is . . . Why?
20. What I would like to learn about in this group is . . .

HIGHEST HOPES, DEEPEST FEARS

OBJECTIVES

I. Behavioral

Members will

1. Identify hopes and fears in writing
2. Interact spontaneously with other group members
3. Practice empathic skills by listening to a partner

II. Cognitive

Members will

1. Decrease sense of isolation by giving and receiving feedback with group members
2. Increase empathy with other members by explaining partner's worksheet

MATERIALS

1. Copy of "Highest Hopes, Deepest Fears" worksheet for each member (p. 48)
2. Ink pens or pencils

METHOD

Group members work independently to identify on the worksheet (copies of p. 48) their highest hopes and deepest fears. After the leader determines that most members are finished, partners are assigned. Partners pair up and discuss their worksheets together. The group then reconvenes in a circle, and each member explains his or her partner's worksheet to the group. Feedback is encouraged.

INSTRUCTIONS

Hand out xerographic copies of the worksheet and instruct members to think about their highest hopes and deepest fears. Tell the group to identify their hopes and fears on the worksheet by writing them out in the spaces provided. After everyone is finished, divide the group into partners, either selected randomly or assigned carefully by design. For example, if Rhonda and Kim have been at odds lately, this might be a vehicle through which differences could be overcome. On the other hand, if you are fairly certain that Rhonda would use this exercise to expose and humiliate Kim, then the two should not be assigned together. Instruct the couples to share their worksheets with one another, making sure they have a good understanding of what their partner means by the material written on his or her worksheet. Encourage partners to question and explore one another's work. This done, call members back to the group circle. Then ask each member to share his or her partner's worksheet with the group. Encourage feedback from the group, although questions and comments should be directed to the presenter of the worksheet, not the author. After this is accomplished, explain that the author now has a chance to comment on how well the presenter understood him or her. Then call on the next member, in round-robin fashion.

CONCLUSION

Conclude the session with some comments about the following:

1. Commonality of hopes and fears expressed
2. Importance of understanding another's perspective (empathy)

AUTHOR'S COMMENT

This exercise has more bang for your buck because two important processes are at work: First, a sense of belonging to the group is promoted when hopes and fears are shared; second, empathic skills are practiced when members present their partner's worksheet to the group.

DYADS

OBJECTIVES

I. Behavioral

Members will

1. Practice social skills
2. Practice assertive skills
3. Identify personality characteristics that need to be changed
4. Identify personality characteristics that are appreciated by others

II. Cognitive

Members will

1. Develop a sense of belonging to the group by interacting one-on-one with each member of the group
2. Enhance self-concept by giving and receiving feedback

MATERIALS

1. Note-sized paper for scheduling interactions
2. Chalkboard or marker board to write questions on (xerographic copies of the questions handed out to members would work equally well).
3. One xerographic copy of blank grid (p. 53)

> NOTE: Room size is important. Participants pair off according to their scheduled "appointments" and interact one-on-one. In a small room, the noise factor can be a killer.

METHOD

In this exercise, each member interacts one-on-one with each other member of the group. The facilitator's task is to schedule the interactions, explain the exercise, and summarize the event at the end of the hour.

To begin the exercise, each member receives a schedule of his or her "appointments," like this:

MATT
1. Chris
2. Melissa
3. Rodney
4. (Timer)
5. Jeremy
6. Jimmy
7. Les
8. Robin

Now, Matt knows that his first interaction is with Chris, his second with Melissa, and so on.

The timer position is used when the grid (p. 53) schedules a group member with himself or herself. When a person is scheduled as a timer, he or she announces the start time for each interaction, allows the appointed minutes to pass, and then calls "Time."

Determining the length of time for each interaction depends on the size of the group. In a group of 8 members, with a session time of 60 minutes, interactions of 6 minutes would be about right, allowing a few minutes at the end of the hour for summation.

Prior to the group hour, the facilitator arranges the names of group members on a grid, as shown in Table 3.1:

TABLE 3.1   Sample Grid for Determining "Appointments"

	M	R	Ma	Je	Ji	L	Ro	C
Melissa	X	1	2	3	4	5	6	7
Rodney	1	X	3	4	5	6	7	8
Matt	2	3	X	5	6	7	8	1
Jeremy	3	4	5	X	7	8	1	2
Jimmy	4	5	6	7	X	1	2	3
Les	5	6	7	8	1	X	3	4
Robin	6	7	8	1	2	3	X	5
Chris	7	8	1	2	3	4	5	X

The X marks the time that the group member is the timer. The grid is a bit misleading in that the leader is the first timer. You will start and stop at the first scheduled interaction. Actually, this position works well because you can model the timer's duties for the rest of the group. Make a xerographic copy of the blank grid (p. 53) each time the exercise is used and the names of members are added.

The timer position will vary according to the number of people in your group. Two or more timers may be scheduled at the same time. Those in the timer position usually enjoy the opportunity to interact spontaneously together while others are involved in their scheduled appointments.

INSTRUCTIONS

At the beginning of the session, tell the group that the importance of peer relationships cannot be underestimated. To use that power, the group hour will be devoted to peer interaction. Each member will have a conversation with every other member of the group.

(Distribute schedules.)

Instruct the group to exchange feedback in completing three statements (write these on the chalkboard):

1. I see you as a person who . . .
2. The thing I like best about you is . . .
3. Something I think you could work on is . . .

Each participant gives his or her partner feedback by completing the three sentences. Explain the role of the timer, and begin.

CONCLUSION

After interactions are completed, take a few minutes to summarize the hour. Discussion questions (following) may be asked by the leader and processed in one of the following manners:

1. If time permits, the questions may be asked in round-robin fashion so that each member has a turn. (This works well with smaller groups.)
2. Discussion questions may be posed to the group at large and answered spontaneously by members.
3. The questions may be addressed to the group as food for thought. No answers are solicited. (This is the usual method, as with groups of 8 to 10, the group hour usually is gone by the time the last dyad is completed.)

Suggested Questions for Discussion

1. How did you feel about giving and receiving direct feedback? Was it comfortable? Uncomfortable? Scary? Embarrassing? Exciting?
2. Which did you like better—giving or receiving feedback?
3. Who usually decided where you would meet—you or your partner? Did you approach others for appointments or did you wait until your partner approached you?
4. Who usually went first—you or your partner? Who decided? Why? How do you feel about that?

5. Did you notice a theme or pattern in the feedback you received? For example, if several members of the group mentioned that you clown around too much, maybe you do.

6. What was the most important thing you learned from this exercise?

AUTHOR'S COMMENT

"Dyads" always rank high as a favored group among teens. That is no surprise, as it has the winning ingredients: structured peer interaction, with little leader input. For that same reason, it's a leader favorite as well. It can be a lifesaver on those days when the thought of facing your group with enthusiasm and energy just about makes you sick. It is a great activity for the therapist who is temporarily out of gas.

Fight the temptation to do paperwork (or anything else) while your group is working. You will miss invaluable cues to members' strengths and weaknesses as they interact with peers. Sit back and watch: It's a good time to practice being quietly available.

TRUST WALK

OBJECTIVES

I. Behavioral

   Members will

   1. Experience a feeling of trust or mistrust or both by allowing themselves to be blindfolded and led
   2. Discuss trust issues in group
   3. Explore trust issues by answering questions

II. Cognitive

   Members will

   1. Increase a sense of belonging to the group by sharing reactions to a group activity
   2. Be introduced to the importance of trust in the group

MATERIALS

Blindfold for each couple. (Colorful bandannas or scarves make suitable blindfolds.)

METHOD

Group members do this exercise in pairs. If the number of participants is uneven, assign the extra person to work with a couple as a threesome.

The pairing of members may be left to the whim of the group. However, it is often useful to assign partners; you may want to break up a clique or promote the interaction of certain members with one another.

The group begins with a general discussion of trust. The trust walk follows the discussion. Each partner has the opportunity both to be blindfolded and led and to be "sighted" and do the leading.

A fairly large area is best. The activity may be outdoors or indoors, as weather and the facility allow. A courtyard or park grounds work nicely, as does a cafeteria, lounge, or day area.

The "sighted" partner leads the "blind" one around the defined area, "introducing" the blind partner to the environment by having him or her feel objects, such as a chair, bush, vending machine, and so on, whatever the environment provides.

At the instruction of the facilitator, the roles reverse, and the blindfolded partner changes places with the sighted one.

Following the activity, the group returns to the group room for processing.

INSTRUCTIONS

Begin the group with a discussion of trust. Some good questions to bring up for discussion are the following:

1. What is trust?
   Assured reliance on the character strength or truth of someone or something
2. Is it good or bad to be trusting?
   Sometimes it's good, sometimes it's bad.
3. When is it bad to be trusting?
   When you are unsure of the motives of the other person—such as strangers or acquaintances who may not be operating with your best interest in mind. (Self-protection should be mentioned as a positive skill.)
4. When is it good to be trusting?
   Focus should be on the here and now: It is good, even necessary, to trust people involved in your therapy, such as your doctor, nurse, counselor, or treatment staff. (Also discuss trust within the group.)

Introduce an exercise that will create feelings of trust or mistrust (or both) right now. Pair up the group and distribute blindfolds. Tell the group that everyone will have the chance to be blindfolded and led and to be sighted and do the leading. Instruct those being blindfolded to be sure they can't see, because seeing really will ruin the experience for them. Admonish the sighted ones to take care of their blind charges.

Allow the couples to make their own decisions about who gets blindfolded first. Watch this decision-making process, and you'll be rewarded with interesting revelations of member dynamics. The behavior of participants as they respond to their blind or sighted roles is equally interesting.

When it seems that adequate time has passed, tell the group to change roles. The one who was leading will now be blindfolded. Terminate the activity when equal time has elapsed, and ask the members to return to the group room.

CONCLUSION

Process the activity by offering the following questions for discussion:

1. What was that like for you?
2. What did you learn?
   Attempt to elicit responses that identify characteristics of trust. Examples: "Elaine talked to me the whole time she was leading me, so it wasn't so scary." "Sam let me walk right into a table! I'm sure I'll trust him again!" "I felt safe because Sarah had both of her hands on my shoulders."
3. Which did you like better—leading or being led?
   Ask this one around the circle so that each member responds. This question opens the door to a discussion of dependence versus independence. Remember to value the perspective of every member. Interesting material comes from this question. For example, a child who has been parentified in the family might prefer being led (taken care of) for a change, whereas teens with control issues much prefer leading.

AUTHOR'S COMMENT

I like this activity because the abstract concept of *trust* is made quite concrete for the group. It also allows the leader to direct the discussion to areas most relevant to a particular group. For example, trust among group members might be the focus for one group, whereas trusting staff may need to be explored in another. If some teens in your group come from particularly unhealthy families, it might be important to talk about the degree to which one should trust in the family. If an alcoholic father makes promises to his child that he seldom keeps, it would benefit that teen to talk about the value of not trusting what Dad says when he is drinking.

PENNIES FROM HEAVEN

OBJECTIVES

I. Behavioral

Members will

1. Give or take pennies from each participant in the group
2. Have pennies given to them or taken away from them by each group participant
3. Discuss feelings about the foregoing two activities
4. Listen to feedback about how they are perceived by peers

II. Cognitive

Members will

1. Identify characteristics in others that promote trust and affection
2. Identify characteristics in self that enhance or discourage trust and affection from others

MATERIALS

50 pennies in a paper cup for each group member

METHOD

Each member is given a cup with 50 pennies in it. Each group member, one at a time, gives or takes as many pennies as he or she wants from each peer, going around the group circle. Then each member takes a turn telling why he or she gave or took pennies from each peer. Processing occurs through discussion and feedback.

For example, if Ginny gave pennies to all of the boys but took pennies from all of the girls, material for discussion seems apparent: Is Ginny simply boy crazy in an age-appropriate fashion? What does her preference for males do to her relationships with females? If she values males so much more highly than she values females, what does that mean in terms of her self-worth? (She is female.) Does she mistrust females? Why?

INSTRUCTIONS

Distribute cups with the pennies in them. Explain that in this exercise, everyone will give pennies to or take pennies from every other member. Proceed in round-robin fashion. For example, start with Michael, to your immediate right. Ask him to go around the group and either take or give pennies, in any amount he chooses, to each member. He starts with Danny, to his right, and gives him 7 pennies. Brent, seated on Danny's right, gets 5 of Michael's pennies. To Danny's right is Katy. Michael takes 17 pennies from her, and so on. Next it is Danny's turn to go around the circle.

After everyone has had a turn, the leader asks each member why he or she gave or took pennies from each particular peer. Encourage members to be as specific as possible. For example, if Barb gave 10 pennies to Mary Beth "because I trust her" or "because I like her," the group doesn't learn much valuable information. If, however, the leader asks Barb to be more specific and Barb says that Mary Beth always smiles at her when they pass in the hallway, or that Mary Beth stood up for her once when she was being teased, or that she liked the way Mary Beth really listened to her, then the group learns characteristics that promote friendship and affection. It is hoped that members will consider trying these behaviors themselves; maybe they will learn what to look for in a friend.

It is particularly interesting when a teen gives away all of his or her pennies or gives away none. A depressed young person or one with the "doormat syndrome" is likely to give away all of the pennies. But so is the rebellious youth with the "tough guy/gal syndrome," who tries to show everyone how unimportant this activity is. Both situations provide grist for the mill. Ideally, the leader can elicit responses and feedback to this behavior from other members. A simple question, such as, "Jamal, what do you think is going on with Jeff that he would give all of his pennies away?" is usually all it takes to get feedback underway.

It is usually no problem to get feedback from the group when one member hoards his or her own penny stash and takes from others. If the group's reaction is harsh, the leader can redirect the focus by suggesting that maybe this member did not have much sense of belonging to the group. The leader then can initiate a discussion about what it takes to feel like a part of a group.

CONCLUSION

Sum up the session by reviewing the positive and negative personality traits that were identified. These may be listed on a marker board or chalkboard during the session; or, at the end of the session, the group can review the characteristics discussed and the leader can list them on the board.

AUTHOR'S COMMENT

This exercise works best with groups whose members are acquainted with one another. I especially like this one for younger adolescents. Preteens around age 11 or 12 are particularly interested in the nuances of peer acceptance, and this exercise helps them identify characteristics that are well received by peers. This is not to say that it doesn't work with older teens, because it can. However, by age 14 to 16, teens often hide their true feelings by giving or taking pennies in equal or near-equal amounts. They don't want to hurt anyone's feelings, so they don't take many risks in this activity. If this happens in your group, develop discussion around "playing it safe" and ask what that means to the group and to individual members.

BUS RIDE

OBJECTIVES

I. Behavioral

Members will

1. Participate in an activity that symbolizes separation of group members
2. Talk about feelings elicited by members leaving the group

II. Cognitive

Members will

1. Explore feelings of separation from the group

> *NOTE:* A coleader is helpful for this exercise. This exercise should be used when several group members are leaving or when the group is terminating.

MATERIALS

Lightweight chairs

METHOD

Members who are leaving the group, or the entire group if this is the last scheduled session, sit in chairs set up as if seats on a bus. (Seats are in the middle of the group circle if several are leaving, or all seats are arranged as if on a bus in the case of a last session.) The coleader signals members to leave, one at a time, as the group discusses separating. When signaled, the members getting off the "bus" walk to a far corner of the room and sit down. After the last passenger has left the bus, the group reconvenes and processes feelings elicited by the exercise.

INSTRUCTIONS

Remind (or announce to) the group that several members will be leaving. Or in the case of a final session for the entire group, announce that this last meeting will focus on separation.

Ask the members to help you arrange the chairs of everyone leaving the group so as to resemble seats on a bus (in twos with an aisle down the middle). Any remaining members place their chairs in a circle around the bus. Members leaving take a seat on the bus. The leader tells the bus riders that they will be signaled to leave the bus when their "stop" comes up. The coleader will tap them on the shoulder to signal their departure, and they will go to a corner of the room or sit against the wall.

The leader initiates a discussion about the members who are leaving or about the group terminating (see "Discussion Guide," p. 62). As the group interacts, the coleader silently taps first one, then another bus rider on the shoulder; that person silently leaves the group. An interval of several minutes should occur between bus stops. After the last rider has taken his or her place outside the bus, a few moments of silence are allowed so that the group can experience the visual impact of the empty seats. Then, the group reconvenes to process the feelings elicited by the exercise.

CONCLUSION

Processing feelings elicited by the exercise provides a good conclusion to the hour. The impact of the empty chairs usually sparks reactions quickly. If the group reconvenes to process things, be sure to leave the empty seats as they are. Sometimes (especially in a small room), I have done the processing right from the members' positions at the end of the exercise; that is, members who are leaving are sitting against the wall or in the corners of the room while others are seated in a circle around the empty chairs, or the whole group is sitting against the walls or in corners.

AUTHOR'S COMMENT

The most powerful experience I have had with this exercise occurred when an entire patient population in a treatment facility for troubled adolescents gathered to say good-bye to eight members of their community who were being discharged. As the bus riders left their chairs, the group discussed what knowing them had meant to the group. One particularly recalcitrant boy ran from the group room in tears in response to expressions of affection and concern from peers on his behalf. It was a breakthrough experience, even though it was his last day in treatment. While the coleader attended this boy, the leader and the rest of the group processed their feelings in reaction to his emotional exit.

DISCUSSION GUIDE

A. When several members are leaving the group:
   1. Let's talk about how we feel about Joe, Sonja, and Chris leaving the group. Perlita, how do you feel about that?
   2. What will it be like for the group when Joe, Sonja, and Chris leave? Will things seem different? How?
   3. Let's give Joe, Sonja, and Chris some feedback about how it was to be in a group with them. Blake, why don't you start.

B. When the group is terminating:
   1. This is our last meeting together. How do you feel about that, Perlita?
   2. What's the most significant thing you've learned as a result of being in this group?
   3. If a good friend asked you what it was like to be in this group, what would you say?

FRIENDSHIP "ROCKS!"

OBJECTIVES

I. Behavioral

Members will

1. Discuss their experience with a positive group and a negative group
2. Observe a demonstration that shows that a collection of rocks is a more powerful force than a single rock (this is symbolic for the power of the group versus the power of the individual)
3. Create a sense of belonging in this group by making a rock necklace or painting on a rock to symbolize group membership

II. Cognitive

Members will

1. Consider the collective power of a group versus the power of an individual by:
   a. listening to the leader's discussion of groups in general
   b. listening to the leader's discussion of positive and negative peer groups
   c. observing a group activity that demonstrates the concepts discussed
2. Consider the positive impact of belonging to this group

MATERIALS

1. A bowl. This can be a mixing bowl of any kind.
2. A rock for each member of the group. Here in the Midwest, rocks with holes in them are plentiful. Many people call them "friendship rocks." I gather the ones I use for this exercise along river beds. (The water has eroded the rock away so that a hole develops.) Friendship rocks are fun to use but not required. If friendship rocks are used, a necklace will be made. If they are not available, select smooth stones that can be painted on.
3. Yarn, twine, or leather thongs if necklaces are to be made

4. Paint and brushes if rocks are to be painted

5. A basket or plastic sack or bucket

6. Water

7. A towel or plastic sheet (to place under the bowl of water)

8. A blackboard or easel (nice but not necessary).

METHOD

When the group convenes, there is a bowl of water on the floor in the middle of the group. The leader asks the group to think about the groups in which they have been members. Then, the leader says a few words about groups in general and peer groups in particular. Both positive groups and negative groups are discussed. (See detailed information for this in Instructions segment.) Each group member identifies a positive and negative group that they have been in if they can.

The leader passes around a basket or bucket with rocks in it. Each member selects a rock.

The leader picks two members to drop their rocks into the bowl of water (one at a time). Then the leader collects all the rocks. This time, the leader drops all of the rocks into the water at once. The difference between what happens when one rock at a time is dropped into the water, and what happens when all the rocks are dropped in is obvious! (Usually, water goes everywhere!)

The power of the group (compared to the individual) has been demonstrated. Now the group makes necklaces out of the rocks or paints on the rocks.

> NOTE: If painting, the group may want to select a special group name to put on the rocks, or they may want to put their own names on the rocks—let them decide.

When the group meets, everyone should wear their necklaces or bring their rocks to place in the center of the group or on some convenient table in the group room.

INSTRUCTIONS

1. Place a bowl of water on the floor in the center of the circle on a towel or plastic sheet

2. When the group convenes, tell them that today, they will be looking at the whole subject of groups and membership in groups. You will also consider and discuss membership in this group.

3. Ask them to list characteristics of a positive group and a negative group. Write suggestions on the board or easel. You may need to help them quite a bit if they are immature. Here's a list:

   A. Positive Groups

      1. Allow you to be yourself; don't make you change who you are to be a member

2. Allow you to disagree

3. Welcome diversity

4. Are supportive when you have problems

5. Allow members to leave if they want to

6. Do not question the loyalty of a member unless the member's behavior transgresses the group's standards of conduct

   B. Negative groups

1. Insist that you think, feel, and behave as the group dictates

2. Do not allow differing perspectives

3. Insist on conformity

4. Are only concerned with the group's agenda (do not encourage exploration of individual issues; i.e., your problems don't matter)

5. Do not allow you to leave

6. May require "proof" of loyalty by insisting members participate in dishonest, dishonorable, criminal, or offensive activities

4. Ask each member to identify a positive group they have belonged to and a negative group they have been in. (Remind them that a family group counts. There are also church groups, clubs and organizations—choir, band, French Club, etc., athletic clubs or teams, school or community theater groups, social clubs, service organizations, scouting and military organizations for teens, cliques [good and bad], and, of course, gangs.) Go around the group round-robin.

5. This is a good time for the leader to point out the possibility that membership in *this* group can be a good thing.

6. Pass the basket of rocks around, instructing each member to choose a rock. I usually ham this up a lot; make a big deal out of how important it is to choose a rock that they really like, one that says something about who they are, one that catches their eye and imagination, and so on.

7. Ask someone to drop his or her rock into the bowl of water (there will be a small splash). Leave that rock in the bowl.

8. Ask someone else to do the same thing (another small splash occurs).

9. Collect everybody's rock, including the two dropped in the bowl.

10. Then, with a great deal of drama, dump all the rocks in the bowl of water at once. **Watch out or you'll get wet!**

11. Invite the group either to make necklaces out of their rocks (if using friendship rocks) or to paint their rocks.

CONCLUSION

While members are either making necklaces or painting, tell them their rocks are symbols to remind them of their membership in this group. Encourage them to wear their necklaces, especially on group days. If they painted their rocks, suggest they put them in a prominent place, such as by their beds, during the week, then bring them to group on group days.

When the painted rocks are brought to group, have everyone place his or her rock in the center of the group circle. It's nice to have a special basket or container in which to place the rocks. This is just another way to emphasize the sense of belonging to a group.

AUTHOR'S COMMENT

The breakdown of the family group and the success of pseudofamily groups (gangs and cults) is known to every professional who works with adolescents. Until responsible adults help young people find positive groups with which to identify, teens will be vulnerable to negative group cultures. If you are using this manual, the importance of the work you do with young people cannot be overemphasized.

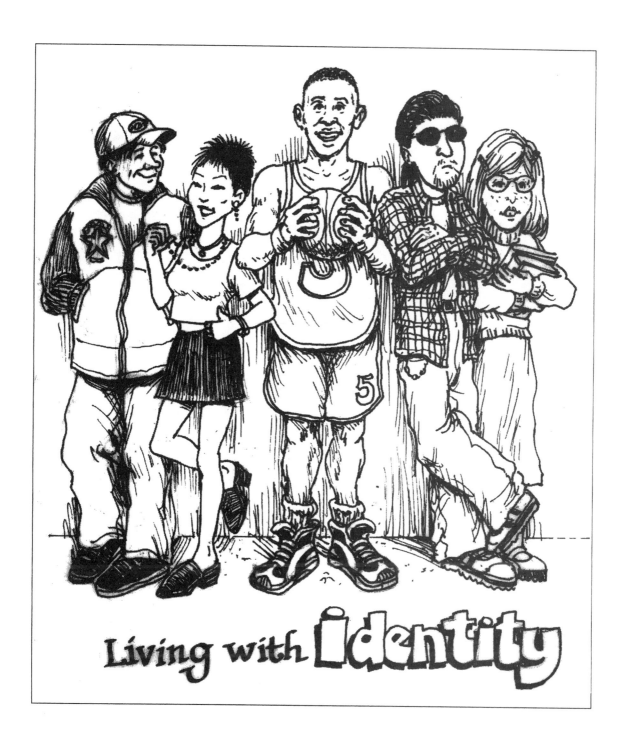

Living with Identity

OBJECTS LIKE ME

OBJECTIVES

I. Behavioral

Members will

1. Choose an object from those provided that is most like them and tell why
2. Listen to others' self-perceptions and give feedback

II. Cognitive

Members will

1. Increase self-awareness by describing themselves in relation to chosen objects
2. Increase self-awareness by listening to feedback from others

MATERIALS

1. Carefully chosen group of objects (objects that have been particularly useful include, but are not limited to, a box of matches, a sponge, a red ball, a clown doll, an old high-top tennis shoe, a mask—Halloween or Mardi Gras—a geode [rock], a pine cone, a puzzle, an eggbeater, a heart-shaped box, and a coach's whistle.)
2. Table for displaying objects

METHOD

The facilitator selects a number of objects such as those suggested in "Materials." Objects chosen should have the potential to elicit certain responses. The facilitator arranges the objects on a table in the middle of the group circle before the scheduled session. When the group convenes, each member, in turn, chooses the object most like himself or herself and tells why. The other group members respond to the self-perception described by giving feedback to that member. Self-perceptions are validated or challenged by the feedback.

ALTERNATE METHOD

If you need to do a group but you don't quite have your act together (you haven't gathered your box or basket of objects yet or, let's say, you forget your basket of objects), there is another way. Each of the group members brings an object from their rooms that is most like them. I've seen everything from articles of clothing to toothbrushes to contact lens cases to stuffed animals used very effectively. This activity works well in inpatient settings. In an outpatient setting, the group members find things they have with them that are most like them. (Contents of purses, pockets, or book bags can be used.) These alternative objects are not ideal choices, but they will work in a pinch.

CONCLUSION

Conclude the session by pointing out that some members seem to know themselves quite well, whereas others are not so aware of what might be motivating them or how they come across to others. If appropriate for your setting, members might be encouraged to discuss this exercise with their individual therapists (or teachers or parents, etc.).

AUTHOR'S COMMENT

This exercise is always *the* favorite. Teens love it, and it offers the therapist an avenue for both validation and challenge.

You will be happiest if you keep your objects all together in one place. I use a large basket; then, there's no last minute panic that sends me scrambling around gathering items.

FISH FOR A THOUGHT

OBJECTIVES

I. Behavioral

Members will

1. Self-disclose by completing unfinished sentences aloud in the group hour

II. Cognitive

Members will

1. Increase self-awareness by completing sentences aloud, spontaneously, in group

MATERIALS

1. Unfinished sentences (cut from xerographic copies of pp. 73-79)
2. Basket, box, or other container

METHOD

Xerographic copies of unfinished sentences are cut out, folded, and placed in a basket or other container in the center of the group circle. Each group member has a turn to "fish" by picking a folded paper from the basket. The member returns to his or her seat and then reads the sentence aloud, completing it in his or her own words. Discussion follows each member's response until the facilitator determines the time to move to the next "fisher."

INSTRUCTIONS

Teens usually respond favorably to a sense of the dramatic, so it's fun to use that by doing something interesting to the basket of sentences. You might put a chair on top of a table in the middle of the group to elevate the basket, for example; or you could place the basket on the floor and cover it with a blue scarf to represent water and, thus, "fishing." You could also decorate the basket of sentences and hand it from member to member. Let your imagination and energy be your guide.

The leader's challenge is to generate discussion around the responses given. Timing is important because, although discussion and spontaneous interaction is the ideal, you need to ensure that all group members have a turn.

Try to elicit the feedback or discussion by posing questions to the group after someone completes a sentence. You may query, "How do you feel about that, Amy?" or "Are you surprised by Steve's response, Yoko?" or "How about a reaction to Juwan's response anyone?"

The sentences are designed to elicit self-disclosing material. The leader's own therapeutic style determines how the material is used.

CONCLUSION

Teens like this exercise for several reasons. First is the phenomenon of being "on stage" that teens both fear and love. The expectation of responding quickly to the unknown sentence heightens their anticipation. Second is the fact that this exercise can elicit material that would otherwise not be shared for lack of an appropriate entrée in the therapeutic setting.

FISH FOR A THOUGHT:
UNFINISHED SENTENCES

(Copy, cut on dotted line, and fold up.)

My biggest fear is . . .

When others put me down, . . .

What I distrust most in others is . . .

I get angry when someone . . .

One thing I really dislike about myself is . . .

I feel sad when . . .

I wish my parents knew . . .

I would like the person I marry . . .

When I like someone who doesn't like me, . . .

If I had to label myself passive or aggressive, I . . .

The hardest thing about being (male, female) is . . .

I wear the kind of clothes I do because . . .

One thing I like about being in this group is . . .

When other people act like my parents towards me, I . . .

One of my most painful childhood memories is . . .

Things would be better in my family if only . . .

One of my scariest memories is . . .

One of the character strengths I like best in myself is . . .

The person in this group that I feel safest with is . . . because . . .

When someone I like does not agree with me, I . . .

When I don't like someone who likes me, I . . .

I like . . .

The happiest time . . .

In school, . . .

I failed . . .

I need . . .

I am best when . . .

I hate . . .

This place . . .

The only trouble . . .

I secretly . . .

Dancing . . .

I can't understand why . . .

I seem to get my way when . . .

The best thing that could happen to my family is . . .

The best thing that could happen to me is . . .

One of the hardest things for me is . . .

When I stand up for myself, people . . .

If I could change one thing about myself, . . .

One thing I admire most in other people is . . . because . . .

What I need most from other people is . . .

OLD ME, NEW ME

OBJECTIVES

I. Behavioral

Members will

1. Express self-perceptions by making collages
2. Share collages with the group
3. Listen as others share collages

II. Cognitive

Members will

1. Conceptualize changes made or desired during therapy
2. Examine undesirable and desired attributes and attitudes in self and in group members

MATERIALS

1. Large sheets of poster board or paper
2. Collection of old magazines
3. Scissors
4. Paste
5. Markers

METHOD

Group members illustrate changes made during therapy by making collages. One half of the poster board represents the "old me," the other half represents the "new me." Pictures, symbols, and words are cut from magazines and pasted onto the poster board. After collages are completed, each member shares his or her collage with the group, and processing occurs through feedback and discussion.

INSTRUCTIONS

Congratulate group members on the important changes that have occurred during their therapy experience. Tell them that this session will focus on those changes. (If new members are in the group or if this is a one-time group for some reason, suggest that participants use the way they see themselves now and the way they would *like* to see themselves.)

Instruct members to cut pictures, symbols, and words from the magazines provided to represent their old me and their new me. Tell them to divide their paper in half with a marker. On one side, they are to illustrate their old me by pasting magazine clippings into a collage; on the other side, they are to do the same for their new me. Tell them they will have about 20 minutes to create their collages and about 40 minutes to process them.

After collages are complete, group members tape them on the wall. When all of the collages are taped up, members take turns explaining their collage to the group.

CONCLUSION

Summarize the session by applauding the changes made by members and by encouraging continued personal growth.

AUTHOR'S COMMENT

This exercise is nice to use near the end of the curriculum because it identifies and emphasizes progress in therapy. However, it may be used anytime by shifting the focus from changes made to changes desired. The exercise works well for all ages, but younger adolescents will need some prompting about personality change, rather than physical change. If you don't help them with that, you will get desired hairstyles, fashion, and material goods. I once had a young boy in group who filled his new me side of the page with cars, stereos, and half-clad women. (Aren't kids great!)

PERSONAL VALUE SYSTEM
AND SELF-ESTEEM

OBJECTIVES

I. Behavior

Members will

1. Identify a personal value

2. Answer a question about that value posed by the facilitator

II. Cognitive

Members will

1. Examine their own value systems

2. Increase understanding of self-esteem

MATERIALS

Chalkboard or marker board for facilitator

METHOD

The format is guided discussion, with the facilitator in a teaching role. The facilitator describes the formation of a personal value system. The group brainstorms to come up with values, which the leader then lists on the board. The rationality of each value listed is explored. The effect of a personal value system on self-esteem is discussed. Alteration of a personal value system is presented.

INSTRUCTIONS

A chalkboard or marker board should be visible to the whole group. Begin by explaining that teenagers are defining and refining their own personal value systems.

1. *Question:* How do we develop a code of ethics or a value system for ourselves?

   Answer: By internalizing messages received from important people in our lives.

2. *Question:* Who would those people be?

   Answer: Parents, relatives, family friends, teachers, ministers, law enforcement personnel, public figures, peers.

   Think about your own values: the "should's and should not's," the "always and never's." For example, most of this group probably would agree that you have a value about honesty. Most of you have "I should be honest" as a value (write this on the board).

3. *Question:* What are some other values? How about you, Sam? (go round-robin around the circle so that each member names at least one value). *Write each member's response on the board.*

The following are common responses (give hints and cues to those who have trouble):

Obey my parents	Don't sleep around	Love your neighbor as
Don't be bossy	Don't trust outsiders	yourself
Don't smoke	Don't have sex before	Always be nice
Don't be selfish	marriage	Always be on time
Don't talk to strangers	Don't cheat	Work hard
Be independent	Don't drink	Be polite
Be a good daughter	Always do your best	Be neat
(son)	Don't lie	Play fair
Finish your job	Go to church	Take care of others
Do well in school	Practice your	Love God
Respect adults	(musical instrument)	Stand up for yourself

Explain that once you establish a value for yourself, it is important that you honor it. If you violate that value, your self-worth goes down. Tread on your own value system, and you'll wind up feeling lousy about yourself. Next, offer a solution. (I do this on the board.)

Explain that, let's say, your value is "Don't have sex before marriage," but you have been having sex with your steady boyfriend. You will feel guilty and bad about yourself unless you do one of these things:

1. Stop having sex with your boyfriend. (Write "Don't have sex before marriage" on the board. [Reinstitute the value.])

2. Decide the value is no longer valid for you. (Erase what you wrote. [Remove the value from your list.])

3. Decide that it is sometimes okay to have sex before marriage as long as you are in a committed relationship. (Rewrite the value as "Don't have sex before marriage unless you're in a long-term relationship." [Alter the value.])

Open the floor for discussion. You may have to address an individual group member or two with specific questions about what comes to his or her mind concerning this value. This dialogue usually gets things rolling.

Everyone should have at least one turn (go around again or take spontaneous entries as the group catches on). Now go back around the circle and question each member's response with something like, "So, Katy, do you always obey your parents?" "Robert, do you always love God?" "Tammy, do you never lie?" "Rasheeta, do you always play fair, even with guys?"

Before going very far, it will become obvious that most of the group violates their own ethical codes at least occasionally. Now, you can focus on how this infraction affects self-esteem.

The violation of one's own value system wreaks havoc on self-esteem. If you have embraced a belief and then go against that belief, your self-concept is attacked. You see yourself as weak, wimpish, no-good, undeserving, unlovable, and so on—all of those things we say to ourselves when we mess up.

CONCLUSION

End the session by reiterating the basics:

1. Part of a teenager's job in life is to develop a personal value system.
2. Self-esteem is tied closely to adherence to one's personal value system.
3. Values from childhood may no longer be relevant. As you grow up, the world becomes less black and white. It is healthful to both examine and change your values as you mature.
4. Values can always be reinstated, deleted, or altered.

AUTHOR'S COMMENT

This exercise is good overall and excellent for offering a way out to sexually active girls who have bought into the "I'm a bad girl" message (although their affect and attitude may not show that). It's also a winner for substance-abusing youth who have lied, cheated, and stolen to support their habit. Reinstating old values after opting for sobriety is both appealing and healing.

HIT PARADE

OBJECTIVES

I. Behavioral

Members will

1. Self-disclose by sharing their favorite songs with the group
2. Practice empathic skills by listening to others and giving feedback

II. Cognitive

Members will

1. Increase self-awareness by explaining why they like the songs they chose and what the songs say about them
2. Increase group cohesiveness and a sense of belonging by sharing thoughts and feelings about a culturally shared interest (contemporary music)

MATERIALS

1. Tape player or CD player for the group
2. Variety of contemporary music tapes or CDs (provided by the individual group members or by the agency or institution)

METHOD

Group members have the opportunity to select and share their favorite songs. Either in round-robin or volunteer fashion, each member plays a favorite song and the whole group listens. After each song is played, the member who chose it explains why it is his or her favorite and what it says about him or her. Feedback from the leader and peers follows.

INSTRUCTIONS

Instructions to the group about this exercise will need to be made prior to the session. Ask the members to find their favorite songs on tape or CD and to bring them to the next group meeting. (Tapes should be wound so that the chosen song is ready to play.)

If members, for whatever reasons, do not have access to tape players or their own tapes or CDs, you will need to provide them. For example, if your group is in an institutional setting where tapes and CDs are not allowed, you will need to make special arrangements. Perhaps a tape player and tapes (or a CD player and CDs) could be provided on a scheduled basis, supervised by program staff. If your group meets in an outpatient setting, members can bring tapes or CDs from home and you can make arrangements to have a tape or CD player available for the group hour.

Give each member a turn to play his or her favorite song as the whole group listens. After the song is played, ask that member what the song says about him or her. Encourage the others to respond and to give feedback.

CONCLUSION

Music is a sacred cow in adolescent cultures and is often an identifying badge of membership in the teenage community. This exercise allows the group members to express personal feelings within the safe context of an acceptable cultural norm. The exercise also provides a forum for the exploration of individual differences in groups where a variety of musical styles may be chosen.

AUTHOR'S COMMENT

I used to do a group using lyrics in contemporary songs to illustrate the perpetuation of gender-based stereotyping. No matter how carefully I presented this material, it was perceived by teens as a criticism of the music. The group session inevitably became a we-you paradigm as members defended the lyrics of popular songs. I finally quit doing that group. The "Hit Parade" exercise is much better because it allows the leader to maintain a totally neutral position in terms of reacting to lyrics or musical style.

NOTE: It is appropriate for the group leader to censor songs with explicitly obscene lyrics. Warn the group, when you announce the exercise, that obscene material will not be acceptable.

T-SHIRTS

OBJECTIVES

I. Behavioral

Members will

1. Share self-perceptions by interpreting artwork
2. Identify aspects of personality that usually remain hidden, and share perceptions with the group
3. Practice empathic skills by listening to others' interpretations and by giving feedback to members

II. Cognitive

Members will

1. Gain insight into their own behavior by identifying their own personality characteristics
2. Enhance a sense of belonging to the group by self-disclosing
3. Enhance self-acceptance by experiencing a nonjudgmental response to shared material

MATERIALS

1. Copy of "T-Shirts" worksheets (pp. 90-91) for each member
2. Colored markers

METHOD

Group members work individually on T-shirts. Hard surfaces are needed; tabletops, floors, and books work well. Members draw their public selves on the front of the T-shirt and their private selves on the back. Each will interpret his or her own T-shirt to the group in round-robin fashion. Group members are encouraged to give feedback to each other.

INSTRUCTIONS

Make two-sided xerographic copies of the "T-Shirts" worksheets (pp. 91-92): the front of the T-shirt on one side, the back of the T-shirt on the other side of the same paper.

You'll find that, inevitably, someone in your group is wearing a T-shirt. Direct the group's attention to the shirt and point out that whatever is found on the front of a T-shirt certainly is meant to be seen. Slogans, advertisements, messages, and famous figures, from musicians to athletes, are displayed proudly.

Point out that one side of their T-shirt worksheet is the front and one side is the back. The front of the T-shirt represents their public self—the self that is meant to be seen. Members are to draw their public selves on the front side of their T-shirts. Drawings may be pictures, symbols, words, or a combination of those. The back of the T-shirt represents the private self—the self that is hidden from others. Using pictures, symbols, and words, each member is to draw the private self.

Suggest that the use of color may help group members illustrate the emotion they're expressing. Ask: "What color do you think of when you think of sadness?" (Some people think of gray or black as the color of sadness; others may think of blue.) "What color do you think of when you think of anger?" "Jealousy?" "Happiness?"

Instruct the group to work individually on their T-shirts. Allow members to move to a comfortable spot to do their work. After about 20 minutes, call "Time" and have the group come together to share their work.

Sometimes, a group may not be finished when the leader calls "Time," and they will ask for more time to work. Explain that it is important that everyone gets a turn to share with the group during the process period and therefore time constraints are necessary. (You may offer 1 or 2 more minutes of production time by using the capitulation to give the group a little control.)

When time is up, call the group back to the circle and begin the processing period in round-robin fashion. When the round robin begins, encourage feedback for the member who just shared his or her work. Statements from the leader, such as, "I think you know yourself pretty well, Joel" or "Ahmed, I had no idea you had so much anger; no wonder you've been bummed out lately!" model nonjudgmental acceptance. Members will follow suit.

CONCLUSION

To summarize this exercise, it's always nice to express appreciation for the honesty expressed by the members in this exercise. Then, be honest yourself. If the group conducted itself honorably by giving each member due respect during his or her turn, say so. If, however, members were only attentive when they were at bat and were inattentive or distracting when others were sharing, let them know. It's a good time to confront narcissism and to point out what it does to the group. Adolescents do not usually understand *narcissism*. They do understand *selfishness* but don't use that word; it's loaded with too many "bad person" connotations. Instead, explain that there are many very good reasons why people become self-focused. A teenager is typically self-focused; it's part of an adolescent's developmental makeup. However, overly self-absorbed people are no fun, make lousy friends, and fail miserably in love relationships. Teenagers understand all of that, and, couched in those terms, they can usually hear the message.

AUTHOR'S COMMENT

It's amazing how much material can be generated in this exercise. It has that "once removed" property that allows self-disclosure rather indirectly.

Religious preoccupation or experience in the occult, as well as physical and sexual abuse, has been revealed (often for the first time) in this exercise.

If you find it necessary to confront narcissistic behavior, remember the gloved hand of humor. It makes for a more comfortable shake than the raw fist of fact.

THE PIPE CLEANER ARTIST

OBJECTIVES

I. Behavioral

Members will

1. Express a self-concept by creating a symbolic representation of themselves with a pipe cleaner

II. Cognitive

Members will

1. Enhance personal identity by using their imagination and creativity to construct a symbol of themselves

2. Experience an authority figure in a nurturing function (reading a story to them)

3. Have the opportunity to increase bonding with the group leader by listening to a heartfelt story

4. Learn something new about other members of the group

MATERIALS

1. Colorful pipe cleaners (large size, found in craft and hobby stores). One pipe cleaner for each group member.

2. A story chosen by the group leader to read

METHOD

The leader reads a story to the group as they use a pipe cleaner to create a symbol with which to represent themselves. The story may inspire a particular symbol, or the symbol may be unrelated to the story. At the end of the story, each group member presents his or her "pipe-cleaner creation" to the group and explains its meaning.

INSTRUCTIONS

The group leader should choose a story that illustrates some desirable virtue, such as honesty, integrity, tolerance, wisdom, and so forth. You might use a fairy tale, myth, or fable. Contemporary stories also make good material for this exercise; check the children's section and the inspirational or self-help sections of your local book store or library. The story should be long enough to allow the listeners to become absorbed but short enough to keep their interest. You might even use several short stories, often found in books of collected stories.

Tell the group you are going to read them a story while they design a "picture" or "sculpture" or "symbol" of themselves with a pipe cleaner. Say that the story you read may or may not inspire their artwork; it's up to them.

After the story is over, ask each group member to share his or her symbol with the group and explain what it means.

CONCLUSION

If time allows, ask the group if they were surprised or particularly intrigued by any member's symbol or explanation. If your group is not very willing to engage in discussion, go around the group round-robin with the question.

AUTHOR'S COMMENT

This exercise usually has a calming effect and is a lifesaver on those days when your group is bouncing off the walls. It is nice to use before bedtime for the same reason. I also like this exercise because it touches on creativity in a more unexpected way—as opposed to the more usual markers-and-paper technique. The story selected may serve as an inspiration for a group member's developing self-concept as well.

STRENGTHS JEWELRY

OBJECTIVES

1. Behavioral

   Members will

   1. Make a list of 5 character strengths they like in themselves
   2. Make a piece of jewelry to wear (bracelet or necklace) that symbolizes the character strengths they like in themselves
   3. Participate in a group activity that involves sharing materials and ideas

II. Cognitive

   Members will

   1. Nurture a positive self-concept by identifying 5 character strengths they like in themselves
   2. Remind themselves of those positive aspects by wearing their symbolic jewelry
   3. Reflect on positive aspects of peers

MATERIALS

1. Paper and pencils for writing lists
2. Leather thongs, wire, string, or other suitable material for making necklaces or bracelets. NOTE: Bracelets are really the best to make because they are easily seen by the wearer; however, they tend to be more difficult to make (due to clasps, etc.). If I use this exercise in individual therapy, I take the client to a local bead store and have the personnel fasten the clasps on. However, if you are more artistically inclined than I am, this may not be a problem. When I do this exercise with a group, I confess to usually doing necklaces, made with leather thongs. I suggest putting knots between beads (or a series of knots) to set each bead off. If you make the necklace long enough, the person wearing it can see the beads.
3. A variety of beads in various sizes, shapes, colors, and materials. (Be sure the holes in the beads are large enough to accommodate the leather, yarn, or twine!)

METHOD

Group members make a list of five characteristics they like about themselves. Then, they select a bead to represent each of the five character strengths they have chosen. They use the five beads to make a necklace or bracelet for themselves. When they look at their special piece of jewelry, they are reminded of five things they like about themselves.

INSTRUCTIONS

Instruct your group to make a list of five things they like about themselves: five character strengths. It is best if each member can come up with the five things, but sometimes, this is too great a task. If you anticipate your group will have trouble identifying "character strengths," help them out. You might prime the pump by asking the group to name some character strengths. Here's a cheat sheet in case you go brain-dead yourself:

smart	optimistic
honest	considerate
dependable	creative
cheerful	polite
mellow	diligent
loyal	kind
funny	nice

Accept other versions, such as good friend, never lie, always on time, do what I'm told, in a good mood, and so on.

There will be some who will list physical attributes. Although eye color is not actually a strength of *character*, if a teen likes her green eyes, I usually go with it. However, four physical characteristics is too many; help that teen identify strengths of character as well as a physical plus or two.

When lists are complete, invite group members to select five beads, one to represent each character strength. Suggest they choose each bead carefully so that each bead chosen reminds them of a specific strength. For example, the most intricate bead might represent "creativity," the yellow bead might represent "cheerfulness," and so forth.

Each member uses the beads chosen in making a bracelet or necklace.

When the group has completed making the jewelry, go around the group round-robin and let each member show his or her creation and identify the character strengths each bead represents.

CONCLUSION

I love this exercise because it forces teens to proclaim their positive traits out loud. For some, it is the first time they have even considered naming their assets. There's a bit of the self-fulfilling prophecy thing happening here, which is just fine. If the little multicolored bead that represents "creativity" can make a teen believe he or she is creative, even just a little, then we have done that child, and the planet, a favor.

Living with Family

FAMILY SCULPTING

OBJECTIVES

I. Behavioral

Members will

1. Demonstrate family dynamics by arranging "family members" in a sculpt
2. Identify possibilities for change by altering or rearranging the sculpt
3. Confront loss issues by placing the lost "family members" in sculpt. (Loss may be by death, divorce, geographic move, or psychological or emotional withdrawal.)

II. Cognitive

Members will

1. Conceptualize family dynamics that may not have been recognized consciously
2. Identify possibilities for change in their families by resculpting their families as they wish they were
3. Enhance self-observation by determining their own "position" in their family

---

NOTE: (A room of adequate size with furniture or an outdoor setting offering a variety of props, such as picnic tables and benches, playground equipment, etc.)

METHOD

Each group member, in turn, is a sculptor. The sculptor creates his or her family as a living sculpt by choosing other group members to represent family members and arranging them in the room so as to symbolize family dynamics.

For example, one girl I worked with chose a boy in the group to be her father. She asked him to stand on a table. Next, she asked the girl selected to be her mother to stand on the floor right in front of her "father." Then, she instructed the father to place his

thumb squarely on top of the mother's head. There was not much question about that relationship as the sculptor saw it!

Ideally, the sculptor chooses someone to stand in the sculpt for himself or herself. This is not always possible when family members outnumber group size. In that case, the sculptor stands in as himself or herself.

After the sculpt is complete, the sculptor interprets his or her work, explaining why family members are positioned as they are.

The leader then invites the sculptor to rearrange the sculpt by making it as he or she wishes it were.

INSTRUCTIONS

Tell the group that in today's session, they will have a chance to be artists—not painters or potters or photographers but sculptors. Explain that each of them will create a living sculpt of his or her family by selecting peers to stand in for family members. Each sculptor will place these family members in the room so that family relationships are expressed.

It is helpful to provide examples. Power and control can be expressed by placing powerful family members above less powerful ones. If Mom has the power, she could be asked to stand on a table. (Sometimes, you will discover that adolescents are aware they have the power when they step up on a table with a knowing grin!) A family member lying on the floor portrays submission or powerlessness. Close or not-so-close relationships can be illustrated by family members' proximity to one another. If an older brother is across the room in the corner with his back to the rest of the family, we know he is not too close to them. However, if he is sitting on Mom's lap, we have another picture.

Usually, adolescents don't need more than an example or two; they are eager to get started. Feel free to make a few suggestions if the first member to sculpt doesn't seem to get it. Often, the first sculptor sets the tone and creates the pattern for the rest of the group, so you want to get the idea across as completely as possible with the first one. For instance, if the first sculptor puts Dad standing next to Mom and starts to move on, stop him or her. Ask whether the sculptor can help the group know more about how Mom and Dad are—Really close? Angry? Bored? Distant? Best friends? They can hold hands if they're best friends, stand with their backs to each other if they're at odds most of the time, or be placed with one above the other if power or control typifies their relationship.

The sculptor must be a part of the sculpt as well. It's best to have the sculptor choose someone else to stand in for him or her. That way, the sculptor can observe the complete family from a distance and perhaps more objectively. If group size makes that tactic impossible, have the sculptor stand in for himself or herself.

Numbers of family members often become an issue. Members will ask how many of their family members to include. Inclusion can be a problem when members have very large nuclear families or in cases where extended family are considered as close as the nuclear family, as in blended families.

Just do what you can do. If the teen who is sculpting has 14 family members and the group size is 8, have the sculptor pick the 8 most important family members, or 9—there's nothing wrong with the leader taking a part. Gender can be a bit sticky with young adolescents. Boys are loathe to assume the part of a girl and vice versa. A sense of humor and some friendly persuasion may do the trick, but don't bank on it. If the only group member left to stand in for someone's 5-year-old sister is a 13-year-old boy who adamantly refuses, use an inanimate object, such as a chair, to be the little sister.

After the sculpt is complete, ask the artist to explain his or her work. Most interaction is between the sculptor and the group leader. The leader may ask questions, make suggestions, and offer interpretations. The leader may wish to challenge the sculptor. For example, statements such as, "Wait, I thought it was more like this . . . " (with explanation or demonstration) can be a valuable intervention.

This exercise allows the leader to "enter" the perceptions of the teenager and to offer alternative perspectives. It's not a good idea to encourage group member interaction, because you usually will run out of time, and time is usually an issue with this exercise. In fact, it's nice to be able to plan on two sessions for this exercise if your group is eight or more. It is such a powerful experience that you will hate to feel pressured by time.

After discussion of the sculpt, invite the sculptor to rearrange the sculpt as he or she wishes it were. Then, discuss that result. At this time, magical thinking can be discovered and confronted. For example, it is very common for children of divorce to recreate their family of origin as intact, as it was before the parents split up. You can ask gently whether this is a possibility. When the sculptor says no, then ask what is possible. The possibility must involve some movement of the sculptor himself or herself. Mom and Dad may never be close again, but the sculptor may see that he or she can move closer to each of them. Emphasize that people have control only over their own behavior. We cannot determine the decisions and behavior of others.

CONCLUSION

It is not necessary to summarize events of this exercise. Conclusions and suggestions come naturally as a part of each member's work.

AUTHOR'S COMMENT

This exercise may be the most powerful one in the manual. There is something about the way all of the sculptor's faculties—the mind, with perception, conceptualization, and fantasy—and the body, with sight, movement, position, and contact—combine to inform understanding of family dynamics. Teens suddenly will see what really is going on in the family through their own efforts to reconstruct it.

In cases where the family is clearly so dysfunctional that nothing the sculptor did could affect the system, identify the teen as a survivor and value his or her coping skills. Coping skills may include escape from the family to the public domain. The Division of Youth Services, Division of Family Services, juvenile court, and so on have many troubled teens who take flight into the system as a survival tactic (although, of course, they may not be aware on a conscious level that they shoplifted or vandalized or ran away in order to get protection from their sick families). In cases where things look really hopeless, ask the teenagers to sculpt the families they hope to have when they have their own families. This feat is a quick way to instill hope and to return the locus of control to the sculptor.

This is the exercise most often extended to two or more sessions so that everyone gets a turn to sculpt his or her family. It is a favorite with teens and staff alike and generally produces a wealth of material to use in other modalities, such as family or individual therapy.

SURVIVAL ROLES IN A FAMILY: A PSYCHODRAMA

OBJECTIVES

I. Behavioral

Members will

1. Participate in structured psychodrama
2. Discuss their family compared to the one portrayed in the psychodrama
3. Identify the role they play in their families

II. Cognitive

Members will

1. Gain awareness of the family as a system
2. Gain understanding of family dynamics in a dysfunctional family
3. Enhance understanding of the dynamics of their own families
4. Enhance self-awareness

MATERIALS

None

METHOD

The leader gives a brief explanation of survival roles that emerge within troubled families. The leader directs a structured psychodrama that portrays a dysfunctional family. Processing occurs when psychodrama participants discuss their roles in the play and their roles in their own families.

INSTRUCTIONS

Give the group an explanation of survival roles that emerge in dysfunctional families. Explain that we learned about these patterns when researchers began studying alcoholics and the families of alcoholics. It was surprising to learn how similar families of alcoholics are. It seems that family members respond to the alcoholism of a parent in very predictable ways. People in alcoholic families believe that they must think, feel, and behave in certain ways to survive in their families. A researcher and author named Sharon Wegscheider-Cruse (1981) defined these "survival roles." Then, we learned that alcoholism was not the only thing that spawned these patterns. Other problems produced the same dynamics. If the problem wasn't Mom's or Dad's alcoholism, maybe it was Dad's gambling or workaholism, or Mom's shopping addiction, or Dad's affairs, or Mom's depression, or Dad's temper and violence. Families organize around these conditions in similar patterns. To illustrate these patterns, the group is going to do a skit.

Explain that you will need most members for parts. It isn't difficult; everyone has only one line to say. First, have the group move all of the furniture to the walls of the room. Next, ask someone to be Dad. For the purposes of this skit, Dad is alcoholic. Encourage members to volunteer for parts; threaten to choose people yourself if no one volunteers. If you are patient, usually volunteers will emerge or the group will volunteer someone. Once you have Dad, ask him to stand with you in the center of the room. Explain that Dad has been a problem drinker for several years and that his drinking has been getting worse every year. Dad's line in the skit is, "I want a drink. I've *got* to have a drink!"

Now, ask for a volunteer to be Mom. Mom joins Dad in the middle of the room. Say that Mom has a sort of blindness about Dad's alcoholism. Allowing herself to know the seriousness of Dad's alcohol abuse is too frightening. It threatens her whole life as she knows it. It threatens her family, her financial security, her emotional security, her relationship with him, her status in the community, everything. Mom's reaction is to pretend that this terrifying specter doesn't exist. Her line is, "Everything's fine. There's no problem here." To depict Dad's lack of emotional strength, ask him to stand behind Mom and to place his hands on Mom's shoulders.

Next, choose the first-born child (male or female, it doesn't matter). Have this child stand next to Mother. This child comes to believe that if he or she is just good enough, the family will be okay. This child is called the family Hero and is an overachiever in almost everything. He or she probably is an excellent student, is a good athlete, holds a student council office, and has a job. The family Hero is dependable and responsible. The family Hero's line is, "It's all right, Mom. You can lean on me." Have the family Hero and Mom link arms.

The second-born child is the Rebel-Scapegoat. When this child comes along, the space for being good is all filled up by the family Hero. The second child believes that he or she can never be as good as the Hero and so finds an identity in being bad. The Rebel's job is to go against family values. The Rebel does poorly in school, chooses the wrong friends, may have trouble with the law, is likely to abuse alcohol and other drugs, and generally stirs up trouble wherever he or she goes. Sooner or later, every-thing bad that happens in the family is blamed on the Rebel-Scapegoat. Actually, this child understands more clearly than anyone else what's going on in the family. The Rebel knows about Dad and is angry! The Rebel's part is to run in a circle around Dad, Mom, and the Hero, shaking a fist and saying, "I hate you, Dad. Get out of my life!" The Rebel is the child most likely to have substance abuse problems or to wind up in a treatment program for acting-out behavior—or both.

The third child in this family finds the situation quite chaotic as he or she grows up. Dad is always gone or drinking or drunk or yelling at Mom and storming around the house. Mom is pretending nothing's the matter, the Hero is busy being perfect, and the Rebel is constantly in trouble. The third child survives by becoming invisible. This child is called the Lost Child. It's the child who is in the bedroom most of the time, plugged into the stereo headphones. It's the child who sits in the back row in every class and never raises his or her hand. It's the child who feels alone in the company of others. Being alone means feeling safe, but it also means feeling lonely. This is the child most likely to be depressed and to attempt suicide at some point. The group member playing the Lost Child will sit in a chair some distance away from the rest of the family. This child has no line to say.

The fourth child in the family is the Sick Child. This child learns that the only safe way to get his or her dependency needs met is through being sick. This child may be the saddest one of all—only feeling worthy when ill. The Sick Child sits on the floor. He or she recites this line while bending over and holding the stomach: "I think I'm going to be sick!"

The baby of the family is called the Mascot. As the name implies, this youngest child receives attention and affection for his or her childish antics and behaviors. The family can gather around this little "bright spot," who distracts them from more serious concerns. The Mascot skips around the family members, pulling on their sleeves or skirts and begs, "Won't you come play with me?"

The last member of this family is optional. If you have enough group members, use her. She's the Mother-in-law, Dad's mother. She stands on a chair and yells at Mom, "It's all your fault!"

Now, you have all of the players, and they know their parts. Have each one recite his or her line to be sure each remembers it. Then explain that, in this drama, everyone says his or her line at the same time. Remind those characters who have an action (the Rebel, who runs around; the Sick Child, who bends over; the Mascot, who skips around; and the Mother-in-law, who points her finger) what they're supposed to do.

It's time to begin. Instruct the players to begin saying their lines and performing their actions when you say, "Go!" Tell them to repeat the lines and actions over and over until you say, "Stop!" Count to three and proclaim, "Go!" Yell "Stop!" when it's clear they have the idea. Usually, the first run-through is tentative and less than enthusiastic. At this point, react like any good director and motivate your cast with encouragement and admonitions. Challenge them to really get into their characters and to feel what those characters feel. Again, begin the drama. Stop it after several cycles and have the group sit down right where they are.

To process this psychodrama, give each character a chance to talk about his or her experience. Ask each one, starting with Dad, what it felt like to play that person. You'll be amazed at how accurately the feelings behind the survival roles will be expressed. A common exchange will sound something like this:

Leader:	What was it like for you to be Dad in this family?
Dad:	I don't know (pause). It felt like I didn't have any control over anything, not me or my family.
Leader:	How did not having control make you feel?
Dad:	Everyone knows dads are supposed to sort of be in charge of things. I think I felt like a failure as a man.

Proceed in this manner until you get to the Lost Child. Skip that character as if you forgot him or her and go on to the Mascot. The group, at some time, will remind you that you skipped the Lost Child. Acknowledge that you did and that that's what happens to the Lost Child in families—they get forgotten, left out. Then process the experience with the Lost Child.

Characteristics of the family roles are provided for the leaders in "Family Roles" (p. 108). This is a useful tool to have nearby so that you don't forget an important point.

CONCLUSION

Ask group members if they saw themselves and their families in this psychodrama. I usually open this up for spontaneous exchange, rather than go around the circle. By now, group members are sitting around on the floor, with perhaps a few who were the audience seated in chairs. The casual positioning lends itself to open discussion.

Questions such as the following usually arise:

Member 1:	Can you be in one role for a while then switch to another?
Leader:	Did that happen in your family?
Member 1:	My brother was the Hero, and I was the Rebel. But when he went away to college, I think I sort of moved to the Hero position. Is that possible?
Leader:	Yes. It's probably because you believed you had "room" to fill that new empty space. Also, maybe you knew, somehow, that your family needed you to be the Hero now.
Member 2:	I think I've moved in and out of more than one role. What does that mean?
Leader:	Tell us about how your family changed. You may have moved into another role because something changed.
Member 3:	In my family, the Lost Child is the oldest. Why is that?
Leader:	Tell us about your family.

AUTHOR'S COMMENT

The leader should have a working knowledge of survival roles and the basics of the adult children of alcoholics concepts.

Expect some uneasiness and resistance as you explain this exercise and the group realizes you want them to take parts in a play. Most adolescents are torn by the desire to be the center of attention and the accompanying terror that they might feel. Silliness and the giggles or sullen mumbling and rolling of eyes are common. Don't despair. Proceed with a positive, confident posture; it's contagious. When you model enthusiasm and the spirit of adventure, your group will respond favorably.

When selecting players for the various roles, it is helpful to assign members to roles you suspect they play in their families. If you have a Rebel in the group, he or she is probably the Rebel in the family. A quiet, shy member who seldom interacts may well be the Lost Child, the silly giggly one the Mascot, and so on. The exercise is even more powerful when a character part mimics the player's real-life role.

Be prepared for almost any reaction to this powerful exercise. Tears, anger, and aha! experiences often are elicited as teenagers recognize their own families or themselves. Support staff may become crucial. A member's individual therapist may need to be alerted to follow up in processing emotions. When I do this activity in schools, I often notify school counselors when a participant seems to need more support. You may need to be available after group for one or two members. It is wise to arrange your time so that your additional counsel is available if needed.

FAMILY ROLES

Members in a shame-based or dysfunctional family often adjust to the stress in the family in different ways. These ways of adjusting have been described by Sharon Wegscheider-Cruse (1981).

Following is Wegscheider-Cruse's description of a chemically dependent family, which applies to any dysfunctional family:

1. *Family Hero:* Sensitive and caring. Feeling responsible for the pain of the family, the Hero tries to improve the situation. The family Hero strives for success, but because the family doesn't change, he or she ultimately feels like a failure.

2. *Scapegoat:* Opposite of family Hero. Tries to gain recognition by pulling away in a destructive manner, bringing negative attention to self by getting into trouble, getting hurt, or just withdrawing. (NOTE: Any attention is better than being ignored.)

3. *Lost Child:* Offers relief for the family by taking care of his or her own problems and avoiding trouble. The family ignores the child. This inattention results in loneliness and personal suffering.

4. *Sick Child:* Finds acceptance and attention in being ill, the only path available for strokes.

5. *Mascot:* Provides relief and humor for the family by being charming and funny during stressful times. This humor does not help the Mascot deal with personal pain and loneliness.

FAMILY MEMORIES

OBJECTIVES

I. Behavioral

Members will

1. Express positive and negative family memories by drawing a positive/ happy family memory and a negative/unhappy family memory
2. Discuss these memories in group

II. Cognitive

Members will

1. Decrease feelings of uniqueness by listening to other group members share both good and bad memories
2. Bring painful memories to consciousness and the light of discussion
3. Reflect on something positive about their family
4. Enhance group bonding by sharing personal information

MATERIALS

Large sheets of drawing paper and colored markers

METHOD

Each group member will draw a happy family memory and an unhappy family memory. Drawings will be shared with the group and the events depicted explained.

INSTRUCTIONS

Pass out drawing paper and markers. Instruct members to divide their paper in half with a dark line. (I feel this is better than using two separate pieces of paper because it illustrates that both positive and negative events occur within a single unit—the paper—the family.)

Tell the group that both good and bad things happen in every family. Ask them to draw a happy memory with their family on one side of the paper and an unhappy memory with their family on the other side.

When the group is finished, go round-robin around the group and invite each member to share the stories represented by what was drawn.

AUTHOR'S COMMENT

This simple exercise is great for young and old alike. The last time I used it was when I was a consultant to management in a community agency. My task was to work on team building with the staff. I was amazed at how quickly the group pulled together during this exercise.

BOY-GIRL RELATIONSHIPS: THROUGH THE FISHBOWL

OBJECTIVES

I. Behavioral

Members will

1. Participate in discussion with same-sex peers
2. Write out questions for other-sex peers about dating and relating

II. Cognitive

Members will

1. Enhance sense of belonging with same-sex group members
2. Increase awareness of sex role stereotyping
3. Increase awareness of other-sex perspective

MATERIALS

1. Pens or pencils
2. Note-sized paper
3. Two small baskets or boxes

METHOD

The exercise uses a fishbowl format: Girls sit on the floor in a circle, with the boys behind them in chairs so that they can look in on the girls' discussion. Then, boys and girls exchange places, and the girls observe the boys' discussion.

At the beginning of the session, boys and girls separate. Same-sex members get together to generate questions for the other-sex group to answer. The focus is on boy-girl dating and relating. The boys' questions to the girls are collected in a basket or box, and the girls' questions to the boys are collected in a separate basket or box. Next, the girls form a circle on the floor, and the boys sit behind them in chairs.

The girls take turns drawing the boys' questions from the basket one at a time. Each question is read aloud, discussed, and answered. Boys and girls change places, and the boys read and discuss questions from the girls.

The facilitator stands back from the fishbowl formation as an observer.

INSTRUCTIONS

Tell the group that today's session offers them a unique opportunity. First, they will be asking the other sex to share their thoughts and opinions on dating and relating. The boys will listen in as the girls read and discuss questions from the boys. Then, the girls will listen as the boys read and discuss questions from the girls.

The boys and girls will get together with one or two same-sex members and think up questions to ask the other group. Leader-provided examples are helpful to get the ball rolling. Good questions to use as examples include the following:

What do you like to do on a date?

How can you tell when someone likes you?

What style of clothing do you like on boys (girls) the most?

Questions should be written on note-sized paper, folded up, and collected. Tell the group to write only one question per piece of paper.

After an ample supply of questions has been generated, collect them, and instruct the girls to sit in a circle on the floor. Tell the boys to sit behind them on chairs (making a circle outside a circle). Begin the discussion part of the exercise with the girls. It works best for two reasons: First, girls are usually more verbal than the boys and quickly turn the answering of questions into an animated discussion. Second, adolescent girls are usually more mature than boys their age. There is less tendency for the girls to devalue the exercise by making fun of it or acting silly. The girls serve as models for the boys' group, which will follow.

Place the basket of questions from the boys into the middle of the group of girls. Instruct the girls to take turns around the circle, drawing a question and reading it aloud. The person reading the question is in charge of discussion of that question. The boys may not contribute to the discussion unless they first are recognized by the discussion leader. Boys must raise their hands and wait to be recognized. After all of the questions from the boys have been discussed or after the girls have used approximately half of the time in the hour, girls and boys change places. Now, the boys read and discuss questions from the girls. Girls may not speak until recognized by the discussion leader.

CONCLUSION

Save about 5 minutes in which to illuminate examples of sex role stereotyping that almost always emerge during this exercise. Challenge the group to think about how preconceptions and prejudice affect the way they think, feel, and behave with the other sex.

Another direction is to summarize by asking the group what came up during the exercise that surprised them or was new to them.

AUTHOR'S COMMENT

Dating and relating to the other sex is like stumbling through fog for most adolescents. It may seem that the only time the light shines clearly is when one makes a mistake—falls into a hole or bumps into a barrier. Then everyone sees! This exercise does not dissipate the fog, but the territory becomes a little more familiar—at least, less mystifying.

SEX: EVERYTHING YOU WERE AFRAID TO ASK

OBJECTIVES

I. Behavioral

Members will

1. Ask, in writing, questions about sex
2. Talk about sexual issues in a mixed-gender group
3. Listen to questions posed by group members and answered correctly by peers or leader
4. Interact with a knowledgeable adult (or adults) about sex

II. Cognitive

Members will

1. Correct misconceptions about sex
2. Receive answers to questions about sex
3. Experience sex as a topic of conversation in a structured, safe environment

> *NOTE:* I do not recommend this exercise for groups of both young and older adolescents. An inexperienced 11-year-old's questions are quite different from a sexually active 17-year-old's. It is an excellent exercise for age-related groups. I've often reassigned groups of mixed ages into age-related groups just for this exercise. If the group members know each other, as in a patient community or school, this exercise works well.

A cotherapist is a must for this exercise (see "A Case for Cotherapy" in Part 2, p. 29). I recommend that both male and female therapists work together, if possible. This is a good time to invite a medical doctor, registered nurse, or other health care provider to sit in as a guest cotherapist if you do not have a medical background.

MATERIALS

1. Note-sized paper
2. Pens or pencils
3. Basket, box, or other container

METHOD

Group members generate questions about sex and write them out on slips of paper. Questions are written anonymously, folded up, and dropped into a container supplied by the leader. The leader draws questions out of the container one at a time, reads them, and answers them thoroughly. Group discussion is encouraged.

INSTRUCTIONS

Distribute paper and pencils. Explain that this session on sex is an offering from the staff (or the therapists) to answer any questions that group members may have about sex. Instruct the group to think of questions about sex and to write each question down on a slip of paper, only one question per slip. Papers then should be folded up and dropped into the container. Have the leader or coleader draw questions from the basket, one at a time, and read them aloud to the group. Give the group at large a chance to provide the answer; if they cannot, the leader or coleader (or both) should answer the question. The questions should be anonymous to encourage more genuine participation. Each question drawn should be answered unless the question obviously is intended to embarrass, humiliate, or gross out the leaders or members or to poke fun at the subject matter.

Members may work on questions independently or may get together with same-sex peers in the group to work on them.

Allow adequate time for group members to generate questions. Then, pass the container around for collection. Reconvene the group in the circle and process the questions.

CONCLUSION

Conclude the session by reminding the group that human beings are sexual beings. Ignoring, discounting, denigrating, or devaluing the sexual side of ourselves leaves us misinformed about who we really are. Knowing, claiming, and respecting our sexuality is essential to total health.

AUTHOR'S COMMENT

This exercise, more than any other in the manual, tests both the scientific and artistic aspects of the therapist. Teenage sexuality is such a loaded subject; factual reproductive information falls short, whereas moralizing falls on deaf ears. It is an arena where mystery and myth rival actuality and factuality in the minds of youth. The therapist who condones open or indiscriminate sexual behavior is irresponsible; the therapist who moralizes is irrelevant. Only a tightrope bridges the gap between minor and mentor.

The following list outlines the usual obstacles to this discussion and offers approaches that may assist the group leader in overcoming them:

1. *The discomfort of such an endeavor propels members of the group into groans, fits of giggles, wide-eyed dismay, or outright hostility toward the leader.* Don't panic; this preliminary outbreak is the group's way of attempting to take control of an uncertain experience. The more unruffled and in control you appear, the more quickly this initial reaction subsides.

Explain to your group that this is an understandably awkward situation. Where else in their lives could such a discussion take place? Probably nowhere. Group therapy provides an environment where boys and girls can talk about some of the things they are most interested in without fear of being judged, or getting in trouble, or having peers think they're weird or ignorant or naive. Group therapy provides adults who know the facts but allows the members to find their own answers.

Tell the group that this group is probably the only place in their whole lives where real questions about sex can be discussed among boys and girls and adults. Focus on taking advantage of a unique experience. It almost always works.

2. *Either the whole group or one or two influential members decide they're above it all.* Common comments in response to the instructions are "I don't have any questions; I already know everything" "I've been doing this stuff since I was 12 years old!" and "This is stupid; what's to ask?"

The best response to this reaction is to appeal to their pride in their intellect. Say that only unintelligent people don't have questions. Smart people give birth to questions in twins and triplets and quadruplets. Tell them you know that none of the group members are "slow." Only those leading the unexamined life would not be writing down questions. It may sound manipulative—it is, but it works.

3. *Questions asked by the group may seem to require moral directives in the answer.* Inevitably, questions about abortion come up. Explain that this is not a forum for questions of morality. Encourage members to discuss those concerns with parents, peers, educators, and spiritual authorities of their choosing. Factual questions about the anatomy and physiology of pregnancy and termination of pregnancy should be answered.

4. *You are not sure of the answer to a question.* Tell the group you don't know the answer but that you'll find out and report back next session.

5. *A question is obviously meant to embarrass or ridicule (is inappropriate).* Don't address it.

Questions about oral sex, anal sex, homosexuality, and masturbation probably will be raised. If these seem like moral issues to you (there is a "right" and a "wrong"), you may not be the appropriate leader for this exercise.

It does seem appropriate that the leader of this exercise make a simple, short statement about his or her own moral convictions. The most responsible seems something like this:

> I do not think that teenagers should be sexually active—that is, have sexual intercourse. It puts young people in emotional situations for which they are not prepared. It is not a question of good or bad; it is a question of emotional maturity. If you are sexually active or if you choose to become sexually active while you are a teen, I do not judge you as bad. I only wish that you make a different choice.

One thing that never fails to amaze me is that the most sexually active teens are also the least informed—or, I should say, the most misinformed. A sample of questions asked by teenagers follows:

Do you have to have intercourse to get pregnant?
What is an IUD?
Do most boys masturbate?
Can you get pregnant during your period?
Why do girls care so much about the size of a guy's dick?
What is oral sex?
How do you know when you have an orgasm?
Why do boys always want girls to give them head?
Do girls have wet dreams?
Where is a clit?
How do guys have sex with guys?
Why is it so hard for girls to get off?
How can you tell when a girl is turned on?
Why does it hurt to have sex?
Why do boys say they love you to have sex with you and then call you a slut?
How do you know if you're homosexual?
Do girls like to have their boobs sucked?
Is it dangerous to your health to swallow cum?
What is PMS?
Why do people have anal sex?
Can you be pregnant and still have a period?
What is blue balls?
How do you use a condom?
What is a tubal pregnancy?
Why do boys toss off all the time?

121

ALTERNATIVES TO ANGER

OBJECTIVES

I. Behavioral

Members will

1. Complete worksheets on anger in group
2. Discuss their own reactions to feeling angry
3. Exchange ideas on healthy ways to deal with anger

II. Cognitive

Members will

1. Explore reactions to anger in self and others
2. Identify healthy and unhealthy reactions to anger
3. Identify false beliefs about anger

MATERIALS

1. Copies of "Alternatives to Anger" worksheet (p. 125) and "False Beliefs About Anger" handout (p. 126) for each member
2. Pens or pencils
3. Marker board or chalkboard

METHOD

Group members complete the worksheet "Alternatives to Anger" independently. Afterward, the group brainstorms to answer the question, "What do you do when you're angry?" The leader writes every technique (both healthy and unhealthy) on the board. Worksheets are processed through guided discussions in group. Copies of the handout "False Beliefs About Anger" are distributed and discussed.

INSTRUCTIONS

Distribute the worksheets. Instruct members to find a quiet spot and to fill out their worksheets independently; allow approximately 15 minutes for this. As the group reconvenes, the leader should ask, "What do you do when you're angry?" List all answers on the board. Encourage participants to think of as many expressions of anger as possible. Common responses include the following:

Get even	Cuss
Hide in the closet	Throw things
Talk to a friend about it	Run
Yell	Do nothing
Ignore it	Go work out
Take a drive	Scream
Hit something (usually the wall)	Hit someone (fight)

Discuss each response with the group and decide whether the response is healthy or unhealthy. Ignoring, "stuffing," or doing nothing is not too healthy nor is reacting in a way that is harmful to self or other.

With this exchange of ideas as a foundation, process the worksheets by discussing each question.

CONCLUSION

Recap the session by naming the "big six" emotions:

1. Mad
2. Glad
3. Sad
4. Scared
5. Guilty
6. Lonely

Reinforce the idea that all emotions just *are;* they are not good or bad. How they get expressed can be good or bad. Challenge the group to try something new the next time they feel angry (try on a new behavior in reaction to anger; be sure it's a healthy one!).

AUTHOR'S COMMENT

Temper tantrums, violent outbursts, and acting-out behavior fueled by anger are common precipitators to both inpatient and outpatient therapy for adolescents. Often, depression and suicidal acting out result from anger directed inward. It would be irresponsible not to explore alternatives to unhealthy reactions to anger when working with troubled teens.

1. When I get angry, I usually (explain what you do)

2. Does this reaction work for me? Why or why not?

3. How is anger expressed in my family?

    Mom:

    Dad:

    Siblings:

    Important others:

4. How can I improve the way I deal with angry feelings?

False Beliefs About Anger

It's not okay to feel angry.

Anger is a waste of time and energy.

Good, nice people don't feel angry.

We shouldn't feel angry when we do.

We'll lose control and go crazy if we get angry.

People will go away if we get angry at them.

Other people should never feel angry toward us.

If others get angry at us, we must have done something wrong.

If other people are angry at us, we made them feel that way, and we're responsible for fixing their feelings.

If we feel angry, someone else made us feel that way, and that person is responsible for fixing our feelings.

If we feel angry at someone, the relationship is over, and that person has to go away.

If we feel angry at someone, we should punish that person for making us feel angry.

If we feel angry at someone, that person has to change what he or she is doing so that we don't feel angry anymore.

If we feel angry, we have to hit someone or break something.

If we feel angry, we have to shout or scream.

If we feel angry at someone, it means we don't love that person anymore.

If someone feels angry at us, it means that person doesn't love us anymore.

Anger is a sinful emotion.

It's okay to feel angry only when we can justify our feelings.

—Author Unknown

THE LOSS CYCLE: A MODEL FOR DISCUSSING DEPRESSION AND SUICIDE

OBJECTIVES

I. Behavioral

Members will

1. Identify personal losses and share them with the group
2. Discuss their progressions through the loss cycle and identify the stages they believe they are in now

II. Cognitive

Members will

1. Gain an understanding of the grieving process
2. Gain an understanding of teenage suicide
3. Either begin or continue to process personal losses
4. Identify factors that may be contributing to depression

MATERIALS

1. Chalkboard, marker board, overhead projector, or easel that can be seen by everyone in the group
2. Copy of "The Loss Cycle" handout (p. 131) for each member

> NOTE: This presentation is based on "The Loss Cycle" model (p. 131).

METHOD

In this activity, the facilitator assumes the role of educator-therapist, as this information is usually new to adolescents. Ideally, members are active participants and are asked throughout the group hour to share their experiences of loss. The model provided enables participants to reframe loss experiences and, it is hoped, to gain comprehension of their own reactions to loss.

INSTRUCTIONS

Ask each group member to think of a time when he or she felt really sad for an extended period of time. Write responses on the board as members share that memory. Common responses include the following:

Someone died.	I left home.
Lose innocence (through rape or incest).	My family moved away.
A friend moves away.	I wrecked my car.
Divorce.	I lost my job.
A love relationship ends.	My girlfriend or boyfriend cheated on me.
Conflict between a friend and me.	
I quit using chemicals.	Lose physical function (through illness or injury).
A brother or sister leaves home.	
A pet dies.	I flunked algebra.

Define these events for the group as "losses." Explain that depression is often the result of a loss. Mention that there are two types of depression:

1. Endogenous
   a. Caused by biochemical condition in the body
   b. May run in families (inherited)
   c. Responds well to antidepressant medication
2. Exogenous
   a. Caused by situation in person's life (often some loss)

Depression often has both endogenous and exogenous features. Now, move to the loss cycle model (p. 131) (Kübler-Ross, 1969).

You will be drawing a skeleton of the model on the chalkboard. Draw a horizontal line, and explain to the group that life proceeds along, "like this." When a loss occurs (make an X at the right-hand end of the line), the lifeline is interrupted, and the individual is propelled into a predictable cycle of reactions (draw a circle looping downward from the X). Recovering from a loss is painful business, however; the process changes a person, makes him or her stronger and more resilient (draw a line coming out of the circle higher than the line entering the circle to symbolize life on a "higher plane").

Ask the group to think about the losses in their lives. Explain that these losses may be old and resolved, the reason they are in therapy, or not yet explored. Ask that each group member share one significant loss with the group. Go around the circle round-robin so that each member has a turn. An attitude of respect and reverence should punctuate the importance of this moment. The leader may lower his or her voice and project an attitude of solemnity.

This accomplished, begin presentation of the model. Frequent questions to the group engage the members and diminish what otherwise would be a lecture format. Questions should be nonthreatening and should invite sharing of experiences. Some useful questions follow:

1. What would you guess is the most usual response (the first feeling you have) to a loss?
   Answer: Denial, shock, disbelief
2. Did any of you react that way to your loss, as if you just couldn't believe it?
3. Bartering usually comes next. Can you think of a time when you thought about bartering in reaction to a loss?
   Example: "Wait! If I work a double shift next week, will you let me keep my job?"
4. What reaction might you guess would follow a period of bartering?
   Answer: Anger?
5. Whom would you be angry with?
   Answer: Person, God, self, others

Fill these in on the board as illustrated on the model.

Usually, teenagers come up with these answers if challenged in an encouraging manner and allowed adequate time.

Proceed through the various stages in a similar manner, challenging the group for answers and welcoming self-disclosure and sharing of experiences.

Spend extra time explaining the phenomenon of "hitting bottom" and exploring the "despair" reaction. Teens who have attempted suicide usually identify readily with feelings of hopelessness, helplessness, despair, and depression.

Teenage suicide is explored easily at this juncture. Again, questions to the group are the best bet.

Suggested Questions for Discussion

1. Do any of you know someone who has attempted suicide? (Or if more appropriate according to the setting, "How many of you have attempted suicide?")
2. Do you think boys or girls are more apt to be successful with suicide? (Boys. They use more violent methods and so are more likely to succeed.)
3. What are some signs that a person may attempt suicide?
   a. The person tells you he or she is thinking about it (suicidal ideation).
   b. The person has planned how to do it.
   c. There is a change in mood from sad or despondent to near happy or happy (a sign of relief because a decision about suicide has been made).
   d. The person gives away cherished personal items (e.g., favorite tapes or CDs, jewelry, clothing).
4. Why is suicide more a threat to teens than to adults?
   a. Teens are more impulsive. They are more likely to act before thinking things through.
   b. Teens do not have enough life experience to understand that time heals many wounds. They may not believe there's a "light at the end of the tunnel."

    5. What should you do if you believe a friend of yours is at risk for suicide? (Tell a responsible adult!)

    6. What should you do if your friend makes you swear you won't tell anyone this secret? (Tell anyway. Narking may save your friend's life!)

After this discussion, it is helpful to explain how some cultures assist people through grieving. Judaism, for example, allows mourners a "time out" from their usual lives in order to get through the business of grieving. Crying, weeping, wailing, pulling hair, and tearing clothing are all acceptable behaviors for mourners in some cultures. Unfortunately, most North Americans are not given permission for such displays of emotionality. Instead, we are encouraged to "be strong" and to "stay in control."

Be sure to value the protections that enable people to avoid the experience of these painful emotions, but also explain the emotional cost of those protections; that is, resolution of the loss may be thwarted by not allowing the strong feelings, such as despair, to be experienced and expressed.

The page illustrating the loss cycle model makes a good handout for appropriate groups. This is a good time to distribute copies.

It's always good to mention that people do not just click through this process, moving from stage to stage without a glitch. Actually, bouncing around the cycle is more like it. For example, it is not unusual to be on the "up" side of the cycle and in the acceptance stage when denial (the very first stage) is reactivated. The person might have been in the stage of acceptance and then find himself or herself thinking, "It just can't be true!"

CONCLUSION

This exercise allows exploration of depression and suicide in a new light. Most teenagers get information on suicide these days. However, not all teens can identify with suicidal ideation or acting out. Presenting information in terms of losses helps all group members identify feelings of depression. Also, this exercise is important because it describes the usual reactions to loss. It may help young people normalize their own behavior in reaction to loss.

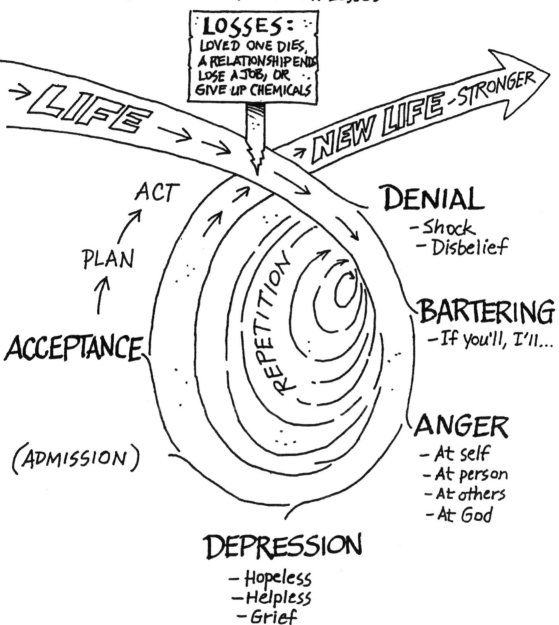

The Loss Cycle

The Normal Cycle for All Losses

LOSSES:
LOVED ONE DIES,
A RELATIONSHIP ENDS
LOSE A JOB, OR
GIVE UP CHEMICALS

LIFE

NEW LIFE - STRONGER

ACT

PLAN

ACCEPTANCE

(ADMISSION)

REPETITION

DENIAL
- Shock
- Disbelief

BARTERING
- If you'll, I'll...

ANGER
- At self
- At person
- At others
- At God

DEPRESSION
- Hopeless
- Helpless
- Grief

THE SHAME GAME

OBJECTIVES

I. Behavioral

Members will

1. Discuss a shame-producing experience
2. Be able to explain the difference between shame and guilt

II. Cognitive

Members will

1. Examine a shame-producing experience in the context of a safe environment
2. Explore their own experience of shame

MATERIALS

1. Envelope for each member of the group
2. Paper clip inside each envelope

METHOD

An emotional reaction (anxiety) is created purposely by the group leader. The reaction is then explored through group discussion.

INSTRUCTIONS

Place an empty chair in the center of the group. Explain that one member of the group will be selected to sit in the chair. That person will answer a list of questions prepared in advance by the leader. The questions will be difficult and quite personal. Group members will have the opportunity to ask questions of the person in the center chair. (Refuse any further explanation.) Announce that the person to be in the center chair will be selected by a random process. An envelope will be passed to each member.

Say that all the envelopes are empty except one, which contains a paper clip. The person receiving the paper clip in his or her envelope will sit in the center chair.

Then, distribute the envelopes with solemnity. In actuality, each envelope contains a paper clip. This way, each member thinks he or she is the "chosen" one. This event should cause some degree of anxiety for everyone.

As the envelopes are distributed, instruct the group not to open them until all are handed out. Now, tell the members to open their envelopes but not to reveal the contents. Wait until each member discovers the paper clip. This done, announce the obvious: Each envelope has a paper clip in it.

Use the remainder of the hour to process the event. The following is a suggested format for processing:

I. Examine the emotional response.
   A. How did you feel when you saw the paper clip?
   B. Think of another time when you had a similar feeling. What happened then?
   C. Did you notice physical signs of anxiety (pounding heart, sweaty palms, butterflies in the stomach)?

II. Examine the belief behind the response.
   A. Why do you think you had the feeling you had? *Common responses:* "People will all be looking at me." "I'll say the wrong thing, and I'll feel stupid." "I don't like being the center of attention because it's embarrassing."
   B. Many of us have irrational beliefs. Do you believe any of these statements are true?
      1. I should never make a mistake.
      2. I must always say the right thing.
      3. Everyone must think I'm smart.
      4. I should never be caught off guard.

   These beliefs are irrational because they're impossible in the human condition (e.g., everyone makes mistakes sometimes; no one always says the right thing).

III. Explore shame.
   A. Shame is the emotion behind the anxiety.
   B. What is shame?
      1. Unplanned exposure
      2. Being IN BARE ASS (embarrass—Yes, teens love this one!)
      3. Feeling bad about who you are
   C. What is guilt?
      1. Feeling bad about what you do (or don't do)
   D. Can shame and guilt be helpful emotions?
      1. Yes. The development of a conscience comes from these emotions.
      2. Discuss people who do not develop consciences. They are usually criminals or antisocial personalities.
   E. Can shame and guilt be harmful emotions?
      1. Yes. They cause unnecessary discomfort with self and restrict personal freedom and a sense of well-being.
   F. What did the feeling you experienced as a result of the exercise do that was harmful or helpful to you?

CONCLUSION

The exercise should have produced an emotion that could be explored through discussion. This activity could be part of a healing process for the shame-based adolescent.

AUTHOR'S COMMENT

You will recognize some basics of Albert Ellis's rational emotive therapy in this exercise. For further information, refer to Ellis (1974).

WORDS THAT WOUND

OBJECTIVES

I. Behavioral

Members will

1. Decrease a sense of isolation and uniqueness by sharing a painful memory with the group

II. Cognitive

Members will

1. Improve self-image by reframing negative messages

MATERIALS

1. Paper and pens or pencils (optional: cassette recorder or player and a blank tape)
2. "Guided Relaxation" (p. 138)
3. "Guided Imagery for Words That Wound" (p. 139)

METHOD

A guided imagery exercise is used to elicit a childhood memory in which hurtful words were said to the participant. These "words that wound" are recorded in writing following the guided imagery. After a brief explanation of internal messages and self-talk, the words that wound are transformed into words that create a positive (rather than a negative) self-image.

INSTRUCTIONS

Tell the group that events of childhood get recorded in our minds in much the same way as a cassette tape is recorded. This tape replays in our minds over and over throughout life. Just as we memorize the words of a song when we hear it often enough, we also memorize the messages on our "memory tapes." Sometimes, these messages are harmful to us. Negative messages can be taped over, just as one can tape over a cassette. Positive tapes help create a positive self-image.

To emphasize and illustrate this idea, you can demonstrate a message being recorded and replayed on a cassette recorder-player. Tape several messages and replay them as the group watches. Suggested messages follow:

"You idiot! Why did you say that!"
"You think you're so smart. Now look what you've done!"
"You're going to make an ass out of yourself in front of the whole group!"

Then, tape over these negative messages with positive ones, such as these:

"Your ideas are good and need to be heard."
"You're just as good as anyone else!"
"Just do it! You'll never know if you don't try!"

Next, announce that you will create a guided imagery experience for the group. This activity will help them get in touch with important events of childhood that have been recorded in memories.

Explain that guided imagery is best experienced in a quiet, relaxed atmosphere. Instruct the group to get comfortable in their chairs or to move to the floor or mats or whatever mode of relaxation your room allows. Dim the lights if possible and read "Guided Relaxation" (p. 138) and "Guided Imagery for Words That Wound" (p. 139) aloud.

After the guided imagery is completed, ask the group to write down the words they thought of during the exercise. Then, go around the circle and process those words with each member. When the member reads his or her message, encourage him or her to transform the message into one that sounds similar but is positive. For example, "You're selfish," a negative image, can be transformed into "You're a shellfish." A shellfish is an animal equipped with its own protective armor—a positive, empowering image. One teenage girl I worked with transformed "You're just a bitch" to "You're pretty and rich." Another changed "You're such a fat ass" to "You've got so much class." A boy changed "You'll end up dead or in prison" to "You'll end up bright like a prism." Another boy who had musical aspirations changed "You'll never amount to anything" to "You're in charge of what you sing." A 15-year-old girl changed "How can you be so stupid?" to "You're full of fun, just like a cupid!" Sometimes, it is hard for members to alter their words alone. Encourage the group to assist in this event. The leader or leaders should become involved if the group falters.

CONCLUSION

End the session by reminding the group that how we think about ourselves affects how we feel about ourselves. The heritage of past hurts can be overcome by the power of positive thinking. Encourage members to practice these new thoughts until they are encoded over the old tapes. Suggest they write out their reframed messages and put them where they are seen frequently, such as taped on their bathroom or bedroom mirror or on the inside flap of a notebook.

AUTHOR'S COMMENT

I think the basis of cognitive therapy, transactional analysis, and inner child work are digested into meaningful concepts for adolescents in this exercise. At best, improved self-imaging is enhanced; at worst, members learn they are not alone in receiving wounds from meaningful (and even well-meaning) family and friends.

GUIDED RELAXATION

I hope you are all comfortable. If you are, close your eyes and pay attention to your body. Allow yourself to be aware of the weight of your body as it rests in the chair (or on the floor, sofa, or mat). (Pause.) Now, I'd like for you to think of your favorite color. Imagine that color is a warm, soft light, cloudlike, that rests around your feet and ankles. Notice how comforting and pleasant your feet and ankles feel in the presence of the light. See the light begin to move slowly up your legs: first, your calves and lower legs and then your thighs and upper legs. As the light moves, your legs can completely relax. (Pause.) Now, the soft light moves through your buttocks, pelvis, and the small of your back. As it moves, you can relax even more, allowing yourself to rest heavily in the chair (floor, couch, mat). (Pause.) The colored, cloudlike light continues to move up your body, through your abdomen, chest, and back. Now, it surrounds your shoulders and neck, allowing the muscles of your upper torso to relax completely. The light moves down your arms, and as you experience its reassuring glow, the muscles of your upper arms, then lower arms, then hands and fingers, can become soft and heavy. (Pause.) The light has a movement. It flows from the tips of your toes, through your feet, and up your legs. It moves through your stomach, back, and chest and around your shoulders. (Pause.) It travels down your arms, through your hands, and right out the tips of your fingers, taking all that stress and tension right along with it. Now, the light flows up through your neck. As it moves across your face, the muscles of your jaw (Pause) and scalp (Pause) completely relax. The light flows right out the top of your head. (Pause.) Now, movement of the soft light is complete; it moves from your toes, up your legs, trunk, shoulders, arms, and hands, and then right out the end of your fingers. It flows up your neck, across your face, through your scalp, and right out the top of your head. You are feeling safe and relaxed in this gentle presence.

(Go right on to the next page.)

GUIDED IMAGERY FOR WORDS THAT WOUND

I'd like you to imagine yourself walking up to a large, ornate gate. It's the gate to your childhood memories. Push through the gate, and hear it swing open. Walk through and hear it click shut behind you. You are on a path that leads to your childhood home. Now, you can see that home. (Pause.) Walk up the steps and look into the window on a scene from your childhood. (Pause.) It's a time when your feelings were hurt. (Pause.) It might be an angry, loud scene, when someone important to you yelled at you with hatred; it might be quieter, when just a small, disapproving remark caused you great pain. What were the words that pierced your heart? (Long pause.) Take those words with you and leave your place of childhood memories. Walk back down the path to the large, ornate gate. Push through the gate, and hear it click behind you. Return to this time, this place, this room.

> *NOTE:* At this point, instruct the group to write out the words that came to them and proceed as described in "Instructions."

SOURCE: The work of David Grove (1991).

LOVE LETTERS

OBJECTIVES

I. Behavioral

Members will

1. Write an affirming message to each person in the group
2. Read aloud to the group the favorite messages received

II. Cognitive

Members will

1. Increase sense of belonging to the group by exchanging personal notes with each group member
2. Increase self-esteem by both sending and receiving notes of affirmation

MATERIALS

1. Enough note-sized paper for each member to have a sheet for every other member in the group (e.g., in a group of eight, each member would need seven pieces of note paper)
2. One envelope for each group member
3. Pens and/or pencils

METHOD

Group members write a positive message to each other person in the group. Each person has an envelope with his or her name on it. Envelopes are handed around, and notes are placed in appropriate envelopes. Envelopes are returned to the addressee and read. Each member shares favorite messages with the group.

INSTRUCTIONS

Instruct members to find a place in the room where they can write comfortably. Distribute paper, a pen or pencil, and an envelope to each member. Explain that each person is to write a *positive* message or note to everyone else. Invite members to tell each other person what he or she likes and appreciates about that person in the note. Notes should begin, "Dear _____ ." They may or may not be signed, as the writer chooses.

Ask each member to write his or her name on the envelope. After most participants have finished writing, have them hand out the envelopes. Explain that the envelopes are to be stuffed with the appropriate notes (Jane puts her message to Robin in the envelope with Robin's name on it, etc.). Then, the envelopes are to be returned to the addressee and the notes read. Last, each member shares favorite notes with the group in round-robin fashion.

CONCLUSION

Conclude the session by reminding the group that affirmation is healing, both when given and when received.

AUTHOR'S COMMENT

This exercise came to me from a patient I worked with in an inpatient treatment facility. Marci was a bubbly, vivacious 16-year-old who struggled with many issues. She was admired by fellow peers and laughingly was considered to be a "handful" by staff. She had done this exercise in a high school home economics class and loved it. She told me she had saved the notes her classmates wrote to her because it had made her feel so good. She thought it would be a good exercise for our Between Teens Group. It was. Marci was killed in a car accident several months after her discharge. This exercise is included in the book in memory of her.

THE WIZARD: A GUIDED IMAGERY EXERCISE

OBJECTIVES

I. Behavioral

Members will

1. Participate in a guided imagery
2. Describe their fantasy to the group

II. Cognitive

Members will

1. Identify and prioritize a personal desire
2. Explore self-worth by identifying a personal asset

MATERIALS

1. "Guided Relaxation" (p. 147)
2. "The Wizard: A Guided Imagery Exercise" (pp. 148-149)
3. Tape player and relaxation cassette (music only)

METHOD

A guided imagery exercise is used to identify deeply held desires and sense of worth.

INSTRUCTIONS

Tell the group that today's activity will be a guided imagery exercise. Explain that the theater of the mind produces important images that can teach us about ourselves. Remind the group that one way to learn about self and others is to share feelings, hopes, and dreams. Therefore, by following the guided imagery, group members will share their fantasies with the group.

Reinforce the idea of control; that is, every member is in control of what and how much he or she chooses to share with the group.

Ask everyone to get as comfortable as possible; this may mean breaking up the circle so that members can move to couches or the floor, or it simply may mean adjusting themselves in their chairs. Darken the room, if possible, and turn on a relaxation tape, if you have one, for background music. Read aloud first "Guided Relaxation" (p. 147) and then "The Wizard: A Guided Imagery" (p. 148-149).

Following the guided imagery exercise, reconvene the group to the circle. Invite each of the members to share the gift they received from the Wizard and the gift they left him. Processing occurs as fantasies are shared and feedback is offered.

CONCLUSION

Summarize the hour by pointing out that our dreams and fantasies can unlock hidden perceptions. It is important to discover the real you; your imagination can help.

AUTHOR'S COMMENT

This exercise often produces information that is difficult to obtain through other avenues. I remember a 15-year-old boy who was not progressing well in therapy. He remained closed and depressed, the cause remaining an enigma to his caregivers. When processing this exercise, he said the gift he chose was a knight in shining armor who galloped in on a huge white horse and carried him away. It was our first clue that the boy was struggling with sexual identity. The boy's individual therapist followed up and learned that the boy had been having a sexual relationship with a young man with whom he was infatuated. The boy felt much shame and confusion about the relationship and had been afraid to tell anyone else about it.

It is common for adolescents with self-esteem problems not to be able to think of anything to leave the Wizard in return. Troubled teenagers often feel so powerless that they don't believe they affect their environment at all. You can use this reaction to point out that one's gratitude and thanks are a powerful response that is adequate in many situations.

Be ready for anything from this exercise: Once, a 12-year-old boy chose a red convertible and a sexy blond from the magic shop. Another time, a 15-year-old girl chose "protection" for her younger sister still at home with an abusive father. (This information led to hotlining the family to state abuse investigators.)

GUIDED RELAXATION

I hope you are all comfortable. If you are, close your eyes and pay attention to your body. Allow yourself to be aware of the weight of your body as it rests in the chair (or on the floor, sofa, or mat). (Pause.) Now, I'd like for you to think of your favorite color. Imagine that color is a warm, soft light, cloudlike, that rests around your feet and ankles. Notice how comforting and pleasant your feet and ankles feel in the presence of the light. See the light begin to move slowly up your legs: first, your calves and lower legs and then your thighs and upper legs. As it moves, your legs can relax completely. (Pause.) Now, the soft light moves through your buttocks, pelvis, and the small of your back. As it moves, you can relax even more, allowing yourself to rest heavily in the chair (floor, couch, mat). (Pause.) The colored, cloudlike light continues to move up your body, through your abdomen, chest, and back. Now, it surrounds your shoulders and neck, allowing the muscles of your upper torso to relax completely. The light moves down your arms, and as you experience its reassuring glow, the muscles of your upper arms, then lower arms, then hands and fingers can become soft and heavy. (Pause.) The light has a movement. It flows from the tips of your toes, through your feet, and up your legs. It moves through your stomach, back, and chest and around your shoulders. (Pause.) It travels down your arms, through your hands, and right out the tips of your fingers, taking all of that stress and tension right along with it. Now, the light flows up through your neck. As it moves across your face, the muscles of your jaw (Pause) and scalp (Pause) completely relax. The light flows right out the top of your head. (Pause.) Now, movement of the soft light is complete; it moves from your toes, up your legs, trunk, shoulders, arms, and hands, and then right out the ends of your fingers. It flows up your neck, across your face, through your scalp, and right out the top of your head. You are feeling safe and relaxed in this gentle presence.

(Go right on to the next page.)

THE WIZARD: A GUIDED IMAGERY

Imagine yourself seated on a bus in a big city. It is a pleasant fall day: The sky is blue and the air is crisp. The sounds of the city traffic, machinery in operation at a construction site, the laughter and taunts of passersby, and the quiet conversation of other passengers on the bus combine to create the background music of a city in motion. Your stop is coming up, and you rise from your seat and get off the bus with several other people. As you walk down the sidewalk, you feel the warmth of the sun and notice the inviting smells from a sidewalk hot dog vendor. Meanwhile, a deliveryman with a dolly piled high with boxes crosses in front of you, and a mother nearby yells at her child to wait for her. As you stand on the corner, pausing while the light changes, you notice an alley tucked between the buildings just across the street. Something is compelling about that alley. You approach it with a sense of anticipation and curiosity.

A simple step and turn from the sidewalk to the alley transports you into another realm. The alley is cool, dark, and deserted. The buildings on either side make a walled passage, slightly narrower than a city street. Trash cans and dumpsters overflow with the week's refuse; a scrawny cat jumps across your path from a nearby pile of over-turned boxes. You are amused with this scene, not frightened. Back entrances to shops and cafes line both sides of the alley, so you are surprised to discover what appears to be the front entrance to some business. A door elaborately painted with once-bright colors of blue and green and orange and purple and red bears a handwritten sign: Kaleidoscope, A Magic Shop. You open the door, and as you step inside, a tinkling bell announces your presence.

The store is dimly lit and smells of dust, like an attic in a very old house. It is difficult to see beyond rows of shelves that are visible through an entryway covered by a beaded curtain.

You are startled by a noise behind you. An old man appears through a curtained doorway behind a counter. He is a curious sight: gnarled and bent like an old apple tree, with a shock of white hair as fine as a cloud drifting around his head. He leans on his cane and looks up into your face. His sparkling blue eyes are like crystal, and his expression radiates warmth.

"Hello," he says, and calls you by name. "I've been expecting you. I am called the Wizard, and you are to select a gift from my magic shop."

He hobbles to the beaded entryway, pulls back the curtain, and motions for you to step inside. As you do, you realize that this is indeed a magic place. Rows of shelving as far as the eye can see extend into the dimness. The shelves go from the floor to heights beyond vision.

The Wizard says he wants you to have a gift. He explains that you are to choose the one thing you want most in life. He says that anything is possible in the Kaleidoscope, but he cautions you to be careful to choose the thing you want most.

You wander down the aisles, exploring the contents of the shelves. Without much trouble, you select your gift (Pause) and return to the Wizard.

The Wizard smiles knowingly when he sees the gift you chose. You are struck with the notion that you must give him something in return for this extraordinary favor, something special that would let him know how grateful you are. You think about what you could give him and make a decision. You give your gift to the Wizard (Pause) and then you leave the magic shop.

You walk back into the now familiar alley, past the back doors of shops and restaurants, past garbage cans and piles of trash. As you walk, your feet leave the pavement and you walk right up into the misty air. You begin to float effortlessly. You float back to this place, this room, this time.

When you are ready, open your eyes and think about your experience and how you might share it with the group.

CARD GAME

OBJECTIVES

I. Behavioral

Members will

   1. Self-disclose by completing the unfinished sentences on the cards drawn

   2. Practice assertiveness by talking in group

   3. Practice empathic skills by listening to others and giving feedback

II. Cognitive

Members will

   1. Self-observe by completing unfinished sentences on cards drawn

   2. Increase sense of belonging to the group by self-disclosing and giving feedback

MATERIALS

Deck of "cards" (made from xerographic copies of Figure 3.14, pp. 152-162; to make a sturdier, more permanent deck, glue the cards on poster board backing)

METHOD

The leader selects one group member to be the dealer. This selection is important, as the dealer position has some degree of power in this exercise. It's a great time to provide a high-status job for a group member who has had little experience as a "chosen one." It can be a low-functioning teen because the job is easy.

The dealer selects a group member for each turn. He or she stands in front of whoever is selected and offers the deck of cards to that member by fanning them out. The player draws a card, and the dealer sits down. The player must complete aloud the unfinished sentence on the card. Discussion about the sentence is encouraged. After discussion is completed, the dealer moves on to the next player.

INSTRUCTIONS

Tell the group that you will be playing a card game. Introduce the dealer you have selected. Instruct the group to select a card from the deck, in turn, and to complete aloud the sentence written on the card. Challenge members to be as honest as possible. Encourage group discussion following each response. For example, the leader may query, "Do any of the rest of you feel the way Jim does at times?" or "What do some of you think Alice meant by that response?" Continue with the game until the session ends.

CONCLUSION

None needed.

AUTHOR'S COMMENT

This is the same format as the "Fish for a Thought" exercise. The presentation is different for variety's sake. Unfinished sentences are a favorite with teens and therapists because they elicit a world of information about group members. Lively discussions often are generated by unfinished sentences. This exercise is included in the "Living With Discovery" section because teens often discover new things about themselves by completing the sentences on the cards. They also discover many things about others in the group through this exercise.

I used to daydream about . . .

My father . . .

It is wrong to . . .

My family . . .

I despise . . .

I've always wanted to . . .

My greatest fear . . .

My mother . . .

Someday I . . .

I am ashamed . . .

I wish . . .

When I disagree with
someone I respect . . .

I like my father, but . . .

At home . . .

If I were a child again, . . .

My greatest ambition . . .

Sometimes I feel like
killing . . .

I could be perfectly happy
if . . .

Most of my friends don't
know that I am afraid of . . .

The big difference between
Mother and Dad is . . .

My greatest mistake . . .

I wish my father . . .

I don't like people who . . .

My family treats me like . . .

My most vivid childhood
memory . . .

What I want most out
of life . . .

I wish I could lose the
fear of . . .

I like my mother, but . . .

I think that a real friend . . .

I still feel bad about . . .

Many of my dreams . . .

One of my favorite things
to do is . . .

The people I like best . . .

Other children in my family . . .

I get mad when . . .

I am afraid to . . .

If my mother would only . . .

When I'm not around, my friends . . .

The worst thing I ever did . . .

When alone, I think about . . .

Some people say I am . . .

I look upon myself as . . . ,
while other people say
I am . . .

What I like best about being a
boy/girl is . . .

When I think about the
most important person in
my life . . .

A MATTER OF PERSPECTIVE

OBJECTIVES

I. Behavioral

Members will

1. Self-disclose by sharing something new about themselves with their group

2. Discuss how they feel when they change the seating arrangement of the group, and/or their posture.

II. Cognitive

Members will

1. Increase awareness of differing perspectives by experiencing a shift in their own perspective

2. Increase awareness of differing perspectives by observing and participating in a discussion about perspectives

3. Increase awareness that the way you view a situation may change the way you feel about a situation by experiencing a change in the group situation

MATERIALS

1. A glass half full of water

2. Paper and pen or pencil for each member

3. One blanket for each small group of three or four

NOTE: Two exercises are offered to make the same point—that perspective is everything. You may want to use both in the same session or split them for use in two sessions.

EXERCISE 1: UNDER THE BIG TOP

METHOD

The facilitator leads a short discussion about perspective, using a glass half full of water as the illustration. In Exercise 1, the leader divides the group into several smaller groups (three to a group). Each small group places a blanket over their heads and has a discussion. After 10 to 15 minutes, the group as a whole reconvenes to discuss the experience.

INSTRUCTIONS

1. Begin the session by asking the group to define the word *perspective*. You'll get answers that come close to what you're looking for: a *point of view*.

2. Next, place the glass of water in the center of the group. Ask the group what they see. Hopefully, some will see the glass as half full of water, and others will see the glass as half empty. Point out that the same glass of water is described very differently by people who see it. Although what is seen (half full or half empty) is quite the opposite of each other, both answers are correct.

3. Then, ask the group to answer the following question in writing on their papers: "You have just received a test back in your English class. You got a C on the test. What do you say to yourself?"

4. After a few minutes, when the group has finished writing, members share their answers in round-robin fashion. Some will say they are happy to have a C; others will be disappointed. This should underscore the example of the half-full, half-empty glass: the same sight or experience can be seen differently, depending on a person's point of view.

5. Divide the group into small groups of three or four. Be intentional about putting group members who do not know each other well, or who have conflict, in the same small group.

6. Instruct the small groups to sit together in such a way that they can cover themselves with the blanket. (The blanket goes over their heads so that each small group is sitting in their own "tent".)

7. Each group has this "Tent Task": *Each person share something about yourself that the others in your tent do not know about you. (You might want to explain that this does not have to be a deep, dark secret. Something such as "I broke my arm in the third grade when I fell out of a tree" or "My favorite color is green" or "The first girlfriend I ever had was Roberta Sanchez" works fine.)* This should take about 15 minutes. Check with your group when things begin to get quiet and see if most are ready to reconvene in the group-at-large format (which probably means blankets are folded, chairs reformed in a circle, and members seated in their original places).

8. Now, go around the circle and have each member answer two questions: *(a) What was it like for you to be in your "tent"? How did you feel? (b) Did you notice anything different about anyone in your tent group?*

CONCLUSION

At this point, you have some choices:

1. You can begin a discussion on how perspective affects everyone. Use examples from your group if at all possible. Generalizing the topic can be equally effective. For example, you might talk about how prejudiced people can be about certain things—people of other races, people who abuse alcohol or other drugs, people with sexually transmitted diseases, people who are poorer or less educated or less attractive—until it happens to them or someone close to them. You might be able to elicit some examples from members once you open this door for them.

2. You can move to the second exercise offered on this topic.

3. You might review what seemed to get accomplished and conclude the discussion. Ideas on what seemed to get accomplished might be something like the following:

A. *Very often, people can choose how they are going to view an event in their lives.* If your girlfriend cheated on you, you can blame the other guy and go after him, you can find some way to get back at her to make yourself feel better, you can steal another guy's girl and prove *you can,* or you can decide that this is pretty normal stuff for teenagers, most couples break up one way or another, and go on with your life as a single person open for new options.

B. *You may decide you do not like someone, when the truth is, you just don't know him or her.* The way you felt about the people in your tent group probably changed. Maybe you felt one way about them in the large group and then felt differently when you were doing your tent task. Ask yourself how you feel about those people now. How do you feel different? Are there new possibilities for friendships? (*For Exercise 2:* Have you ever found that sometimes people become more attractive when you get to know them? It's as if you "look at" them differently. Does anyone have an example of that?)

C. *A change of perspective can change a situation.* Marty wanted to be in the in-group more than anything. She focused all her energy on doing things that she thought would please others in the popular group. She dressed like them, talked like them, liked who they liked, and despised who they despised. It was not working. She still was not accepted, and she felt sad and lonely. So Marty, with some help from her school counselor, changed her perspective. She let go of having to be in that particular group and began looking around for other girls she found interesting. She also decided just to be herself. In no time, she had new friends and a new attitude. The in-group was still around, but they no longer had power over Marty. Has anything like this ever happened to you?

AUTHOR'S COMMENT

I find that the kids tend to feel a closeness and have somewhat of a bonding experience with the others in their tent. The environment of the tent sets the groups apart. Words like "family," "club," or "team" have been used to describe the feeling. If your kids have trouble putting words to this dynamic, you might want to suggest what you think you are seeing. This helps the group learn to articulate relational or emotional events.

EXERCISE 2: IT'S AN UPSIDE-DOWN WORLD

METHOD

The facilitator leads a short discussion about perspective, using a glass half full of water as the illustration (if not used with Exercise 1).

In Exercise 2, the leader and members will end up lying on the floor with their legs and feet in their chairs. Then they will discuss the changed perspective they now have of the group experience. Either continue, or begin, some of the discussion offered in the preceding exercise. The point is, *a person's point of view* (perspective) is a powerful tool: (a) If you can see the other person's perspective, you may feel differently about the situation, or (b) if you can change your perspective, you might be able to change your situation.

What is really rich is if the group has been processing something important, some problem. Maybe the problem concerns a group member, either with others in the group or in his or her own personal situation. Or it might be a problem the group is having. Perhaps, the problem is with school rules or some authority figure, such as a teacher or principal. Likewise, if the group is in an in-patient or group home setting, the problem could be with facility rules or personnel. Use this as grist for the mill. *Talk about these things, then try the following:*

INSTRUCTIONS

(Omit 1-4 if used in same session as Exercise 1.)

1. Begin the session by asking the group to define the word *perspective*. You'll get answers that come close to what you're looking for: a *point of view*.
2. Next, place the glass of water in the center of the group. Ask the group what they see. Hopefully, some will see the glass as half full of water, and others will see the glass as half empty. Point out that the same glass of water is described very differently by people who see it. Although what is seen (half full or half empty) is quite the opposite of each other, both answers are correct.
3. Then, ask the group to answer the following question in writing on their papers: "You have just received a test back in your English class. You got a C on the test. What do you say to yourself?"

4. After a few minutes, when the group has finished writing, members share their answers in round-robin fashion. Some will say they are happy to have a C; others will be disappointed. This should underscore the example of the half-full, half-empty glass: the same sight or experience can be seen differently, depending on a person's point of view.

5. Get out of your chair and lie on the floor with your legs in the chair. You are now looking at the ceiling. Invite the group to assume this position. Usually, there will be giggles and comments—not always. Ask them what seems different about being in the group. (You're looking for what they see, how their body feels, what interests them at the moment, etc.)

6. Now, ask how they feel about the conversation preceding the change of position. They may have trouble with this, so be ready to help them. Suggest that maybe the issue being discussed suddenly feels less important. Maybe it doesn't seem so pressing now. Maybe the energy each member was putting into the problem seems a bit much from this perspective. Could it be that it is possible to reduce the impact of a problem by changing the way one views it?

CONCLUSION

See Conclusion of Exercise 1.

AUTHOR'S COMMENT

I have had good luck with this exercise in individual therapy as well. Sometimes, it's just the twist needed to get a kid who is "stuck" to see another perspective.

THE BLACK BALLOON:
PROBLEM IDENTIFICATION

OBJECTIVES

I. Behavioral

Members will

    1. Identify and discuss specific personal problems in group

II. Cognitive

    1. Identify specific personal problems

    2. Differentiate between problems over which they have control and those in which they do not

MATERIALS

    1. One black balloon for each member of the group (not blown up)

    2. Name tags for each person

    3. Scotch tape

    4. Markers

    5. Straight pins

METHOD

Group members make name tags and tape a straight pin to the name tag. (The rationale behind this is to connect the pin—which becomes a decision-making tool—to the person's name, to underscore a sense of ownership of the decision.)

Next, the leader does some teaching about problem identification. Each member tells about problems in his or her life. The leader helps them identify problems over which they have some control and those in which they do not.

Black balloons are passed out to each member. Each person blows up his or her balloon, using one breath to represent each problem they have. The balloons are tied at the neck and the leader discusses the choices one has in confronting problems.

Following the discussion, members may or may not choose to pop their balloons with the pin from their name tags.

INSTRUCTIONS

1. Instruct group members to make a name tag for themselves. Encourage them to personalize their name tags by being creative. Ask them to secure a straight pin on the front of their name tags with a small piece of tape.

2. Pass out balloons.

3. Ask them to think about the problems in their lives. Cue them by saying it might be problems with their parents or siblings. It might be problems at school with teachers or coaches. It could be problems with friends. There may be problems with a girlfriend or boyfriend. Perhaps there are problems with the law.

    Talk about the two kinds of problems: those we can do something about and those over which we are powerless. For example, a teen who has temper outbursts can learn to control his or her behavior; but a child is powerless over his parents' decision to divorce. It is important to distinguish between those problems we can do something about and those we cannot. Elicit examples from the group by asking (something like): In your own life, what is a problem you can do something about and what is one you can't? I like going around the group round-robin with this one so each member does some problem identification.

> NOTE: This may help you recognize members who have not identified or cannot identify problems. Sometimes, kids come from such dysfunctional families, or have so much trouble in school or with peers, that they are overwhelmed. They may not be able to separate specific problems from what seems like a huge undifferentiated mass. If you see evidence of this in a group member, you may want to do some individual work outside of group with that teen on problem identification.

4. Black balloons are passed out to each member. Invite members to blow up their balloons, using each breath to represent a problem they have. One problem is "blown" into the balloon with each breath. If only one or two problems are identified, tell that member to blow the problem(s) into the balloon over and over again. Eventually, each member should blow up his or her balloon to capacity and tie the neck in a knot. Now, they have their own personal "black balloon of problems."

5. Tell the group that at this point, they each have a choice. They can begin to work on those problems over which they have control and let go of those over which they have no control or not. It's up to them. If they would like to continue

carrying around their black balloons of problems, they may choose to do so. If, however, they decide to take action (by accepting responsibility or by letting go), they can remove the pin from their name tags and pop the balloons. Bang!

CONCLUSION

It is good to follow up the exercise and reinforce the concept if possible. You might want to spend another group session working on problem identification (and resolution) or use the group exercise as a platform from which to jump into some good individual work.

AUTHOR'S COMMENT

The exercise is complete in and of itself, but I have found the visual impact of the black balloon an especially useful tool in continued work on problem identification and resolution. All I have to do is remind the teen of that black balloon, and he or she "gets it." Just say something like, "Are you going to carry that black balloon around some more, or do you want to get rid of it?"

CHEMICAL DEPENDENCE:
THE DISEASE CONCEPT

OBJECTIVES

I. Behavioral

Members will

1. Demonstrate understanding of the disease concept of chemical dependence by answering questions

II. Cognitive

Members will

1. Explore their own feelings about chemical use and abuse

MATERIALS

1. Story "Ted's and Jane's Big Adventure" (pp. 177-178)
2. Presentation guide—Table 3.2. Diabetes and Chemical Dependence: A Comparison (p. 175)
3. Discussion format guide—Table 3.3. Discussion Format for Marker Board, Chalkboard, or Transparency (p. 176)
4. Marker board, chalkboard, or overhead projector

METHOD

The group leader orally presents information that compares diabetes and chemical dependence by using Table 3.2., Diabetes and Chemical Dependence: A Comparison (p. 175) as a presentation guide. (NOTE: To present the information in written form, see Table 3.3 [p. 176])

Following this short presentation, the leader chooses a group member (or asks for a volunteer) to read "Ted's and Jane's Big Adventure" (pp. 177-178). The narrator reads the story. Afterward, he or she acts as discussion leader by asking the group to answer the questions that follow the story.

INSTRUCTIONS

Tell the group that chemical dependence is today's topic and ask them why they think a "Living With Chemicals" section is a part of the Between Teens Group curriculum. (Answer: Because the majority of people will establish some kind of relationship with alcohol and other drugs during their teenage years.)

Present the disease concept of chemical dependence by using the presentation guide (Table 3.2). Use the discussion format guide (Table 3.3) for display of discussion material. After your presentation is complete, either choose someone in the group to read "Ted's and Jane's Big Adventure" (pp. 177-178) or ask for a volunteer. (NOTE: Be sure that whoever is narrator reads well; the story is lengthy.) Ask the narrator to lead a discussion by using the "Questions" and "Suggested Questions for Discussion."

CONCLUSION

Wrap up the session by asking the group what, if anything, they learned that was new. Check in with each member. I also like to ask for reactions to the idea of chemical dependence as a disease.

AUTHOR'S COMMENT

Teens seem to like this session because it deals with chemical use and abuse in a nonjudgmental way.

TABLE 3.2   Diabetes and Chemical Dependence: A Comparison

Diabetes	*Chemical Dependence*
1. Diagnosed by a set of symptoms: polyuria (urinate frequently), polyphasia (always hungry), polydipsia (always thirsty), weak or shaky, sweats	1. Diagnosed by a set of symptoms: use of MAC (mood-altering chemical), denial (of problems with MACs), problems in family, problems in relationships, physical problems, emotional problems, legal problems
2. Progressive illness: will get worse if untreated; terminal illness (death)	2. Progressive illness: will get worse if untreated; terminal illness (death, prison, psychiatric institutionalization)
3. Genetic predisposition: The more family members with the illness, the more likely the chance you'll have it, too	3. Genetic predisposition: The more family members with the illness, the more likely the chance you'll have it, too
4. No cure but can be controlled	4. No cure but can be controlled
5. Control involves active participation of sufferer.	5. Control involves active participation of sufferer.
6. Control implies responsibility on the part of the diabetic: knowledge of disease, knowledge of treatment regime: diet, medication, support groups.	6. Control implies responsibility on the part of the chemically dependent: knowledge of disease, knowledge of treatment regime: abstinence, AA/NA (support groups), psychotherapy.
7. The diabetic is not responsible for having the disease. The diabetic is responsible for controlling it.	7. The chemically dependent is not responsible for having the disease. The chemically dependent is responsible for controlling it.
8. Diabetes can be caused by an underlying physical disorder: pancreatitis, cancer of pancreas.	8. Chemical dependence can be caused by an underlying emotional disorder: depression, bipolar disorder, personality disorder.

TABLE 3.3   Discussion Format for Marker Board, Chalkboard, or Transparency

Diabetes	*Chemical Dependence*
1. Symptoms	1. Symptoms
_____	_____
_____	_____
_____	_____
_____	_____
2. Progressive	2. Progressive
3. Genetic predisposition	3. Genetic predisposition
4. Cure? No. Control? Yes.	4. Cure? No. Control? Yes.
5. Victim must act	5. Victim must act
6. Responsibility implied	6. Responsibility implied
7. Blameless	7. Blameless
8. Underlying disorder	8. Underlying disorder

TED'S AND JANE'S BIG ADVENTURE

Ted and Jane graduated from high school in May. Both planned to go to State University in the fall. Ted is diabetic and on insulin. Jane is chemically dependent and is involved in a local AA group for young adults.

Ted found out he was diabetic when he passed out at a soccer match in his freshman year and was taken to the hospital. Jane admitted she had a drinking problem during her sophomore year when she passed out at a party and then wrecked her car later that night on the way home. Both were hospitalized at City Hospital. Ted spent 8 days in the Endocrine Unit and attended daily classes for diabetics. Jane was a patient in the Substance Abuse Unit for 28 days and attended groups and lectures every day.

Although Ted and Jane didn't know each other very well, both were invited to a Fourth of July party given by Buzz, a mutual friend. His parents owned a lake house on Clear Water Lake. They also had a ski boat and a swimming dock. Buzz's parents were in Europe for the summer. Jane and Ted were fired up for this party! The girls were instructed to bring the food; the boys were to bring the alcohol. Jane made her "to-die-for" double chocolate brownies. Ted got his older brother to buy some Ever Clear so that they could make a batch of Purple Passion.

The Fourth turned out to be a perfect day: bright and hot. Everyone piled in their cars; a few put down their convertible tops, others opened their sun roofs, and everyone blasted their stereos. The trip to the lake took about an hour. On arriving, coolers, picnic baskets, and swim bags were unloaded. Then, everyone headed for the boat dock. The boat was on the first ski run of the day by 11:00 a.m.

Ted, an avid water skier, had trouble waiting for his turn to take a run. He hung back for the sake of politeness but quickly got sick of watching others fly across the water. Finally, when most of the group were breaking for lunch, Ted had a chance to go out. As he fought with the tangled rope and clumsy skis in the water, it flashed across his mind that he had not done his blood test that morning and had completely forgotten to take his a.m. insulin. This fleeting realization was wiped away as the ski rope, now taut, pulled him forward. He responded automatically, positioned himself in the water, and yelled, "Hit it!" After a great run that lasted 20 minutes, Ted was picked up and was on his way back to the dock. Eating, drinking, and merrymaking were the order of the day.

Jane, in the meantime, had been fighting a familiar war on the battlefield of her mind. Although none of her friends pushed alcohol in her direction, the fact that it was all around her was hard to take. She watched as her friends drank and laughed and seemed to be having so much more fun than she was.

Jane wanted to be a part of it all and decided that a couple of beers, after all of these months of abstinence, wouldn't hurt.

Ted began to feel weird and shaky. He thought it was because he'd had a long, hard ride on the water and he'd probably burned up all the calories of his breakfast-on-the-run. He figured he would be fine after he ate something. The dock was loaded with coolers and baskets of food—everything from fried chicken and chocolate cake to ham sandwiches and deviled eggs. Ted's thoughts raced, "I deserve a day off that stupid diet. For once, I'm eating and drinking everything everyone else is!" Jane's double chocolate brownies were outstanding. An hour later, after eating a huge plate of forbidden food, Ted didn't feel very well. No one seemed to notice how strange he felt. He decided to go up to the cabin and . . . everything went black.

Ted's passing out seemed to put a lid on the party atmosphere. Several guys rushed him to City Hospital while one of the girls called his parents. "Some kind of diabetic crisis or coma," the doctor said.

Jane didn't want anything changing the high *she* was on. The "couple of beers" had become a six-pack by the time the guys got back from the hospital. They reported that Ted had almost gone into a diabetic coma. The doctor said he was out of danger now and his parents were on their way. Everyone was relieved. Now, it was time to let the party continue!

Mixing Purple Passion seemed a good way to jump-start a party atmosphere. Jane found a plastic dishpan under the kitchen sink. Someone brought grape Kool-Aid®, and Ted's Ever Clear was on the kitchen table. Five minutes later, the "brew" was mixed. Jane was aware of the soaring, rocketing buzz that caught her and carried her to that old familiar place of oblivion. At first, she felt in the center of things as the music blasted and she joked and laughed with friends. Later, it was more like she was the observer, watching herself from some distant place. What was she doing in the bedroom with Chuck? Maybe it didn't really matter—or did it? Some physical pull was in charge; she could only stumble along with it. She was aware of the weight of Chuck's body on hers, the smell of his hair, and a feeling of exposure, shame, and then it all went black . . .

Questions

1. Who was responsible for Ted's diabetes? For Jane's alcoholism?

   Answer: No one; the conditions are diseases.

2. Who was responsible for Ted's coma? For Jane's blackout?

   Answer: Ted and Jane. They did not take care of themselves, and they knew how to do that.

3. Where did Ted go wrong?

   Answer:

   a. Belief that he could "beat the system," that he was invulnerable (wouldn't suffer consequences)

   b. Skipped his a.m. insulin

   c. Went off his diet

4. Where did Jane go wrong?

   Answer:

   a. Belief that she could "beat the system" (control her drinking) and that she was invulnerable

   b. Started drinking

5. How could Ted have managed his disease in this situation?

Answer: Complied with medical regime by taking a.m. insulin and sticking to his diet

6. How could Jane have managed her disease in this situation?

Answer:

a. Not taken the first drink of alcohol; other beverages available to drink (e.g., soda pop, iced tea)

b. Not have gone to the lake party, as she knew alcohol use would play a major part

Suggested Questions for Discussion

1. What new information did you learn from this story?
2. How would you feel if Ted and Jane were your best friends?
3. *For boys:* How would you feel if Jane were your girlfriend? *For girls:* How would you feel if Ted were your boyfriend?
4. Is it possible to "party" responsibly?

BETWEEN TEENS PLAYHOUSE:
THE RISE AND FALL OF ONE GOOD GUY

A Skit to Illustrate the Progressive Nature of Chemical Dependence

OBJECTIVES

I. Behavioral

Members will

1. Participate in a play production by working on a set and/or taking a part in a short play

II. Cognitive

Members will

1. Explore the progressive nature of chemical dependence by:
   a. Illustrating their concepts of *normal, euphoria,* and *pain* on poster board and discussing how these emotional states change as the chemical dependence progresses
   b. Participating in (or observing) a short play
2. Increase sense of belonging to the group by working together on a project

MATERIALS

1. Three poster boards
2. Colored markers or paints
3. Copy of "The Rise and Fall of One Good Guy" for each group member (pp. 183-185)

METHOD

Group members work together to create "sets" for a short play. Three poster boards are used to illustrate *normal, euphoria,* and *pain* as emotional states. Posters are drawn and discussed by group members. Posters are placed in chairs or taped on a wall to provide the set for each of the three scenes in the play. The leader assigns the parts for the play, and group members perform the play (reading their parts from the script provided).

INSTRUCTIONS

Tell the group that a play will be produced and performed during this session. Divide the group into three subgroups and provide each subgroup with a poster board and colored markers or paints. Assign to each group the task of illustrating an emotional state: Group I, normal; Group II, euphoria; and Group III, pain. (Alternative procedure: Having each group member draw on each poster board works well for a small group.) Teens often balk at this assignment; drawing a feeling state seems too abstract at first. Encouragement from the facilitator is usually all that's needed. You might say: "Of course, you can! Use your imagination!"

After the poster work is completed, go around the group (round-robin) and have each subgroup explain its drawing. Tie the discussion of these feeling states to the progression of chemical dependency by pointing out that as dependence to chemicals progresses, a shift occurs: What once was a normal state followed by euphoria followed by pain becomes a pain state followed by normal with no euphoria.

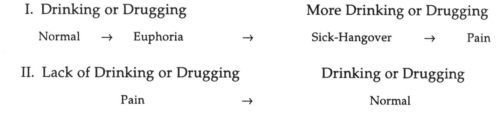

Ask group members to talk about their own experiences with normal, euphoria, and pain states. Encourage them to express what being high was like for them. Ask them how they felt when they came down from a high. Usually, if the leader adds no lecturing, moralizing, or opinion giving at this point, the teens will end up telling each other about the physical and emotional cost of using chemicals.

After discussion of the posters is concluded, use the posters as sets for the play. Either tape them on a wall, spaced far enough apart so that the play participants can move from one set to the next, or stand them up on chairs placed at intervals around the room.

Next assign play parts: Narrator, Mike, Sara, Doug, and Amber. No rehearsal is necessary; the cast can read their parts from the script provided. Extra group members serve as the audience.

CONCLUSION

Ask each player what it felt like to be that character. Encourage discussion after each response.

AUTHOR'S COMMENT

This exercise is a powerful way to educate teens about the progressive nature of chemical dependence. Lectures and presentations by adults do not engage most teens on a personal level.

If the play does not fit the group you are working with, rewrite the script yourself. For example, with inner-city youth it might be more appropriate if the football game was changed to a well-known meeting place and the cheerleader character was at work or baby-sitting rather than cheering at the game. You could have the characters smoking dope instead of drinking alcohol, if that is the drug of choice among those in your group.

THE RISE AND FALL OF ONE GOOD GUY

Characters

Narrator

Mike

Sara

Doug

Amber

Scene I (the cast in front of the "normal" poster):

Narrator: It's a cool, crisp Friday afternoon in October. The final bell just rang its announcement that the weekend has begun. Mike, a freshman, approaches a group of his friends in the school parking lot.

Doug: There you are, Mike! I couldn't find you after class. What did you think of old man Ferguson's test?

Mike: It was about what I'd expected; I should get at least a B.

Doug: Easy for you to say! I thought it sucked!

Amber: Are you guys coming to my house after the game tonight? Mom and Dad are gone for the weekend, and I'm having people over.

Mike: This is perfect! I wasn't excited about another boring Friday night. I'm sick of the football-game-followed-by-cruising-Main-Street routine. Doug, will your brother make a liquor run for us?

Doug: Probably. Stan's usually cool about that. I'll stop by his place on the way home. He should be there because he's working graveyard shift tonight. You guys will have to come up with the money first, though.

Amber (*addressing Mike*): Are you going to bring Sara? I've kind of lost track. Are you on-again or off-again?

Mike: I lose track myself, but you know how Sara loves to party. I'll call her. She'll go.

Doug: Kickoff is at 7:30; we'll pick you up around 7:00.

Mike: You guys can suffer through the game if you want. As for me, I'm for forgetting the game and starting to party early. How 'bout it? We've got Stan to buy for us. Let's make the most of the night!

Amber: It's A-OK with me if we start early. Because Sara is a cheerleader, she can't come until after the game, but most of the rest of us can.

Mike: I could stand to get really wasted! I'm sick of school already, I'm sick of fighting with Sara, and I'm sick of my parents hassling me! I'm ready to P A R T Y; see you there!

Scene II (the cast in front of the "euphoria" poster):

Narrator: It's a sunny Sunday afternoon in May, 5 years later. John and Beth, high school sweethearts, are getting married. Their wedding has been a good excuse for a reunion of the old group. The friends are visiting at the wedding reception, which is being held at a local hotel banquet room. Among the guests are Sara and Mike, who had gotten married after high school graduation.

Amber *(to Doug):*   I don't know how Sara can stand the way Mike has been acting. He's been half smashed all weekend! It isn't cute anymore. I feel sorry for her. You can tell how embarrassed she is.

Doug: Well, with a baby on the way, she must feel pretty trapped. Can't you say something to her, Amber?

Amber: I don't think I can because she acts like nothing is wrong. She's never said a word to me about any problems between her and Mike.

Sara *(Sara pulls Mike away from the crowd so that she can speak to him privately):*   Mike, please! Don't drink anymore! If you would just look around, you'd see that nobody else is getting wasted. This is a formal wedding party!

Mike: See, Sara. You said it yourself—party! We haven't been with these people for a couple of years; it's cause to celebrate! Anyway, you're wrong. Everyone is drinking. I think *you're* the blind one.

Sara: I didn't say they weren't drinking. I said they weren't getting . . .

Mike *(interrupts):*   Oh, cut me some slack, Sara! It's been hard to live with you since you've been pregnant. That's the *real* problem! First it's PMS, then it's pregnancy. You just look for ways to criticize me when you get in your bitchy moods! No wonder I drink! Anyway, baby, you know how hard I work. I deserve to be able to play hard too. It's the only real fun I have.

Scene III (cast in front of "pain" poster):

Narrator:	It's 10 years later. Mike and Sara have a brand new house. Their two children—Jeremy, age 9, and Travis, age 7—are spending the weekend at Grandma's because Mike and Sara are having a big party. It's almost Halloween, and a Halloween party seemed a good way to entertain friends and show off the new house at the same time.
Doug:	Sara, your house is beautiful, and the party is wonderful! I'm amazed we've come this far since high school. To tell you the truth, though, I always knew Mike would be successful. Speaking of Mike, where is he? I haven't even seen him for the past hour!
Sara:	Oh, he's around here somewhere. You know Mike—always circulating . . .
Amber *(approaching Doug and Sara):*	Sara, I think you should give Doug the prize for best costume! Any guy with the guts to dress like Minnie Mouse deserves it . . . even if he is my guy!
Doug:	You should have seen the kids when they saw me in this costume. Ben just cracked up, and Annie said, "Daddy looks like a girl!" Well, I'm going back for more of that clam dip.
Amber:	I do love your house, Sara. You and Mike seem like the perfect couple!
Sara *(bursting into tears):*	Oh, Amber!
Amber:	Let's get you some privacy.
Sara *(in the bedroom now):*	I'm leaving Mike. Amber, I can't stand it anymore.
Amber:	I assume you mean his drinking.
Sara:	Oh, yes! I don't have the energy to pretend and cover up for him anymore. He manages to function at work, but that's the only place he functions!
Amber:	Doug and I have been worried for a long time, Sara. I don't really know how you've stood it this long. Mike has become a miserable person, hasn't he?
Sara:	Yes. He used to be such fun. That's part of what I loved about him! Now it's just awful. Nothing seems to make him happy. Not even the drinking! And I can't let him ruin the kids' lives. They're seeing what's happening; they know what's going on.
Amber:	Does Mike know you're leaving?
Sara:	I don't think so. I've threatened to leave several times, but he always promises he'll quit. He can't quit, though, Amber! Now I don't care anymore. It's going to kill him. He's losing me, the kids, the house, everything!

REFERENCES

Berkovitz, I. H., & Sugar, M. (1975). Adolescent psychotherapy, group psychotherapy, family psychotherapy. In M. Sugar (Ed.), *The adolescent in group and family therapy* (pp. 3-23). New York: Brunner/Mazel.

Carrell, S. E. (1991). *Between teens groups.* Unpublished master's seminar paper, Southwest Missouri State University, Springfield.

Ellis, A. (1974). Rational emotive therapy. In A. Burton (Ed.), *Operational theories of personality* (pp. 308-334). New York: Brunner/Mazel.

Grove, D. (1991, May). *Healing the wounded child within.* Seminar presented to professional therapists in St. Louis, MO.

Kübler-Ross, E. (1969). *On death and dying.* New York: Macmillan.

Rogers, C. (1961). *On becoming a person: A therapist's view of psychotherapy.* Boston: Houghton Mifflin.

Scheidlinger, S. (1991, April). *Group treatment of adolescents in school, clinical, and hospital settings.* Seminar presented to professional therapists at Menningers Institute, Topeka, KS.

Wegscheider-Cruse, S. (1981). *Another chance: Hope and help for the alcoholic family.* Palo Alto, CA: Science & Behavior Books.

ABOUT THE AUTHOR

Susan Carrell, RN, MS, LPC, is a therapist in private practice (Carrell Counseling, P.C.) in Springfield, Missouri. She is the Episcopal Chaplain for Southwest Missouri State University, Drury College, and Ozarks Technical College. Previously, she was a substance abuse counselor for adolescents in an inpatient treatment facility and a psychiatric nurse clinician for hospitalized adolescents. She was owner and director of a state-certified alcohol and drug education program for youth. She has also facilitated groups for high-risk adolescents in the Springfield public high schools.

· · · · · · · · · · · · · · · · · ·

ABOUT THE ILLUSTRATOR

· · · · · · · · · · · · · · · · · ·

Jack Wiens, MA, LPC, is a therapist in private practice with Columbine Behavioral Consultants in Frisco, Colorado. He also is a freelance artist and does fine art painting.